# DERBY
# TO
# STOKE-ON-TRENT

## Vic Mitchell and Keith Smith

**MP** Middleton Press

*Front cover: The cooling towers of the closed Willington Power Station form the backdrop to this view of no. 56105, which has just left the Derby to Burton main line on its journey west to Grangemouth. The tankers have come from the Rolls Royce sidings at Sinfin, south of Derby, on 12th June 2014. (J.Whitehouse)*

*Back cover: The Railway Clearing House map for 1913 features the complexities at Burton-on-Trent. Our route is covered on its 1947 edition.*

*Published September 2016*

*ISBN 978 1 908174 93 2*

*© Middleton Press, 2016*

*Design      Deborah Esher*
*Typesetting Cassandra Morgan*

*Published by*
        *Middleton Press*
        *Easebourne Lane*
        *Midhurst*
        *West Sussex*
        *GU29 9AZ*
*Tel: 01730 813169*
*Email: info@middletonpress.co.uk*
*www.middletonpress.co.uk*

*Printed in the United Kingdom by Henry Ling Limited, at the Dorset Press, Dorchester, DT1 1HD*

# CONTENTS

# INDEX

# ACKNOWLEDGEMENTS

We are very grateful for the assistance received from many of those mentioned in the credits, also from A.J.Castledine, G.Croughton, G.Gartside, J.Horne, S.C.Jenkins, N.Langridge, B.Lewis, J.P.McCrickard, T.Walsh, and in particular our always supportive families.

I. The Railway Clearing House map for 1947. The two blue sections shown on the back cover were connected by through trains regularly.

# GEOGRAPHICAL SETTING

The Stoke-on-Trent and Cheadle districts are above the North Staffordshire coal measures, while most of the route passes over extensive deposits of limestone mixed with clay. Much of this proved ideal for making china and the Stoke area has long been known as The Potteries. Further east, mudstones and sandstones prevail.

The high ground over which our route passes is drained to the south into the River Trent, whereas the water flowing north reaches the River Mersey. The Trent & Mersey Canal was built to link the two areas and the railways followed.

Our journey starts close to the River Derwent in the county town of Derby and then becomes close to the River Trent, near Willington. South of here, the River Dove flows into the Trent and we then run close to the former, to Uttoxeter. Needwood Forest is on the south side of the Dove Valley, but the district is largely agricultural.

We travel in Derbyshire until reaching the River Dove and then pass into Staffordshire.

The maps are to the scale of 25ins to 1 mile, with north at the top, unless otherwise indicated.

# HISTORICAL BACKGROUND

The 1839 Birmingham & Derby Junction Railway was linked to Stoke-on-Trent by the North Staffordshire Railway in 1848 - west of Uttoxeter on 7th August 1848 and east thereof on 11th September 1848. The Act was dated 28th June 1846.

The line ran north from Burton-on-Trent and a direct east-west link through Egginton was added by October 1849. Stoke also received lines from the north and from the south in 1848. An east-west link north of Burton was opened in 1849 and a line north from this to Mickleover was in use from 1878 to 1990, it being operated by the Great Northern Railway initially.

The NSR ran north from Uttoxeter in 1849 to Rocester and beyond; this line lasting until 1965. A route southwards to Stafford was in use from 1867 until 1951. It became part of the GNR.

The NSR became a constituent of the London Midland & Scottish Railway, when the grouping took place in 1923. The GNR then became part of the London & North Eastern Railway. The line north of Burton lost its local trains on 1st January 1949 and all services in 1968. Freight closures are given in the captions.

Upon nationalisation in 1948, the LMSR was largely allocated to the London Midland Region of British Railways, while the LNER entered the Eastern Region.

Privatisation brought Central Trains to operate the route from 2nd March 1997. London Midland was the franchisee from 11th November 2007.

## Burton Branch

As stated, this was originally part of the main line, but only for about a year. For most of the life of the line it was operated as a branch from Tutbury. The intermediate stations were closed in 1951 and the service ceased on 11th June 1960.

Gradient Profile for 1970.

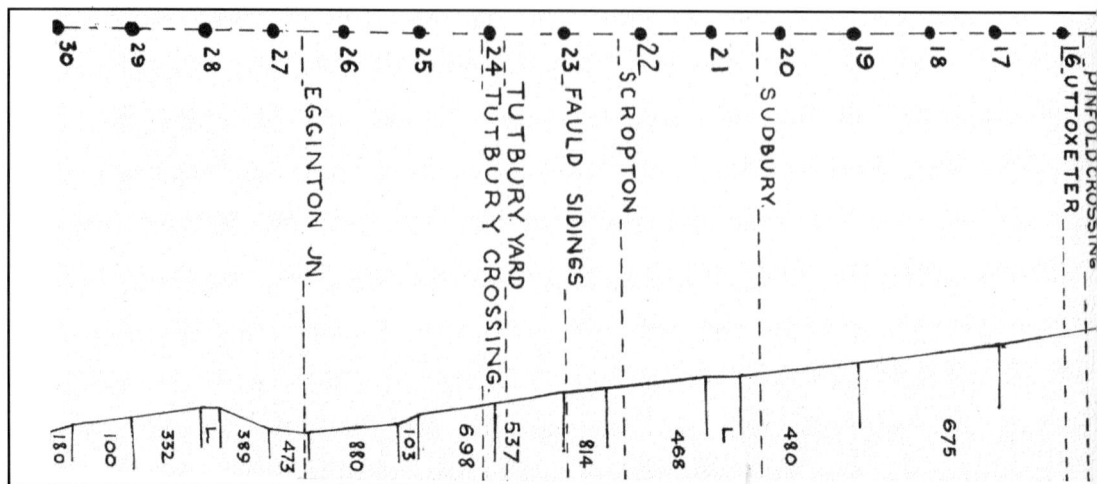

## Stafford Branch

The GNR opened this route from Bromshall Junction, on the NSR, on 23rd December 1867. It carried passengers between Stafford, Uttoxeter and Derby Friargate until 4th December 1939. The goods traffic continued until 5th May 1951, but longer at Stafford Common.

## Cheadle Branch

This was opened east from Cresswell by the Cheadle Railway for one mile on 7th November 1893. The route was completed on 1st January 1901. The one intermediate station was renamed Tean in 1907 and the line became part of the NSR in 1908. A 2½ mile diversion was completed in 1933 on the 3¼ mile long branch. This was needed to avoid Cheadle Tunnel, which had become subjected to severe settlement.

The branch closed to passengers on 17th June 1963, general freight continued until 1978 and mineral traffic until 1986.

# PASSENGER SERVICES

The weekday train frequencies shown in the tables below refer to those running on at least five days per week. The table omits short runs at the Stoke end of the line, which were once numerous. While there were some through trains on the Burton Branch, most ran as a shuttle service from Tutbury. The Stafford Branch was the former GNR route and most trains originated from Derby Friargate or beyond. Some of the trains on the Cheadle Branch ran to and from Stoke, to supplement its suburban service.

## Main Line

|  | Weekdays | Sundays |
|---|---|---|
| 1869 | 5 | 2 |
| 1901 | 8 | 3 |
| 1933 | 11 | 5 |
| 1956 | 8 | 5 |
| 1990 | 16 | 8 |

## Burton Branch

|  | Weekdays | Sundays |
|---|---|---|
| 1895 | 10 | 3 |
| 1910 | 11 | 3 |
| 1927 | 16 | 4 |
| 1947 | 8 | 2 |
| 1959 | 7 | 0 |

## Stafford Branch

|  | Weekdays | Sundays |
|---|---|---|
| 1869 | 4 | 0 |
| 1899 | 6 | 1 |
| 1924 | 4 | 0 |
| 1938 | 4 | 0 |

## Cheadle Branch

|  | Weekdays | Saturdays | Sundays |
|---|---|---|---|
| 1893 | 7 | 8 | 2 |
| 1902 | 5 | 5 | 2 |
| 1922 | 4 | 5 | 4 |
| 1927 | 4 | 5 | 0 |
| 1939 | 2 | 5 | 0 |
| 1946 | 2 | 3 | 0 |
| 1948 | 3 | 3 | 0 |

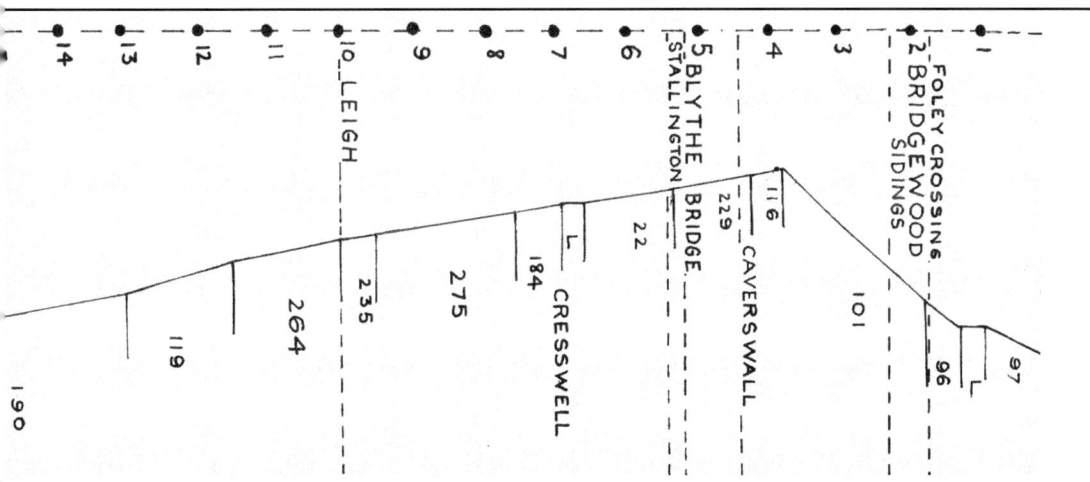

## STAFFORD and UTTOXETER. [Gen. Man., J. Bucknall Cooper, Stafford.

| Miles. | Down. | gov mrn | 1&2 exp | gov aft | Sats. only. | gov aft | gov b | |
|---|---|---|---|---|---|---|---|---|
| — | Stafford dep | 7 45 | 1125 | 1 20 | | 4 5 | 6 25 | .... |
| 4¼ | Salt ........ | 8 0 | a | 1 35 | | 4 15 | 6 40 | .... |
| 5¾ | Weston 159 | 8 5 | 1135 | 1 40 | | 4 20 | 6 45 | .... |
| 7½ | Stowe..[158 | 8 10 | .... | 1 45 | | 4 25 | 6 50 | .... |
| 10 | Grindly[159 | 8 18 | .... | 1 53 | | 4 33 | 6 58 | .... |
| 15 | Uttoxeter a | 8 30 | 1155 | 2 5 | | 4 45 | 7 10 | .... |

| Miles. | Up. Bridge St., | gov mrn | gov aft | Sats. only. | gov aft | gov aft | gov aft |
|---|---|---|---|---|---|---|---|
| — | Uttoxeter d | 9 0 | 1220 | | 2 40 | 5 15 | 7 45 |
| 5 | Grindley.... | 9 12 | 1232 | | 2 52 | 5 27 | ... |
| 7½ | Stowe..[158 | 9 20 | 1240 | | 3 0 | 5 35 | 8 3 |
| 9¼ | Weston 159, | 9 25 | 1245 | | 3 5 | 5 40 | 8 7 |
| 10¾ | Salt....[111 | 9 30 | 1250 | | 3 10 | 5 45 | 8 12 |
| 15 | Stafford125, | 9 45 | 1 5 | | 3 25 | 6 0 | 8 25 |

a Stops when required.

June 1869

## DERBY and BURTON to CREWE & MACCLESFIELD.—North Stafford.

Coaching Supt., Charles Lockhart. Goods Man. and Canal Supt., Edward Pamphilon.

| Fares. | | | Down. | Week Days. | | | | | | | | | Sundays | | |
|---|---|---|---|---|---|---|---|---|---|---|---|---|---|---|---|
| s. d. | s. d. | s. d. | St. Pancras Station, | mrn | aft | mrn | mrn | aft | aft | mrn | mrn | aft | aft | aft | aft |
| .... | .... | .... | LONDON 166 ..dep | .... | 8 35 | .... | 6 15 | .... | .... | 10 0 | 1145 | 3 0 | 8 35 | Sat. | .... |
| .... | .... | .... | 164 ,, (Euston) ,, | .... | 7 0 | .... | 7 30 | .... | .... | 6 25 | 11 0 | 12 0 | 7 0 | | .... |
| .... | .... | .... | NOTTINGHM 174 ,, | mrn | 7 10 | 7 50 | 1020 | .... | .... | 1225 | 3 20 | 5 45 | 7 0 | .... | .... |
| .... | .... | .... | LEICESTER 166 ,, | | 6 30 | .... | 1012 | .... | .... | 1218 | 2 35 | 5 37 | 7 0 | .... | .... |
| 1 cl. | 2 cl. | 3 cl. | Fm. Boston, Grantham, | 1,2,3 | 1,2,3 | 1&2 | 1&2 | 1,2,3 | 1,2,3 | 1,2,3 | gov | 1,2,3 | gov | 1,2,3 | 1,2,3 |
| s. d. | s. d. | s. d. | &c., pp. 110, 99, & 174. | mrn | a c | exp | a | aft | aft | i | h | fast | mrn | aft | aft |
| .... | .... | .... | Derby ..........dep | | 8h0 | 9g0 | 1110 | .... | | 1g45 | 4e15 | 7e10 | 8 50 | .... | 5 30 |
| 1 3 | 0 11 | 0 7 | Eggington .......... | | 8 16 | i | h i | .... | | .... | 4 31 | a | 9 6 | .... | 5 46 |
| .... | .... | .... | 177 PETRBRO' (G.N.) dp | | .... | .... | 6 35 | .... | | 1032 | 1236 | .... | .... | | .... |
| .... | .... | .... | LEICESTER 177. ,, | | 6b0 | .... | 9 20 | .... | | 1220 | 2550 | .... | 7 0 | | .... |
| .... | .... | .... | Burton ........dep | | 8 5 | 9gj0 | 1110 | .... | | 1g50 | 4e25 | 7e15 | 8 55 | | 5 35 |
| 1 10 | 1 5 | 0 11 | Tutbury .......... | | 8 26 | 9 20 | 1132 | .... | | 2 7 | 4 41 | 7 31 | 9 15 | | 5 55 |
| 2 5 | 1 9 | 1 2 | Sudbury.......... | | 8 34 | .... | Wd. | .... | | 2 15 | 4 50 | 7 39 | 9 24 | | 6 4 |
| 2 8 | 2 0 | 1 4 | Marchington ........ | | 8 40 | .... | .... | .... | | .... | 4 56 | .... | 9 31 | | 6 11 |
| .... | .... | .... | Uttoxeter Junction .. | | 8 50 | .... | 1145 | .... | | 2 24 | 5 3 | 7 48 | 9 38 | | 6 17 |
| 3 2 | 2 4 | 1 6½ | Uttoxeter (Bdg. St.) | | 8 55 | 9 33 | 1149 | | | 2 29 | 5 7 | 7 51 | 9 43 | .... | 6 22 |
| 4 1 | 3 1 | 2 0½ | Leigh..........[158 | | 9 8 | .... | .... | | | .... | 5 19 | .... | 9 53 | .... | 6 36 |
| 4 8 | 3 6 | 2 3½ | Cresswell .......... | | 9 17 | .... | .... | | | 2 47 | 5 27 | 8 6 | 10 4 | .... | 6 44 |
| 4 11 | 3 8 | 2 5½ | Blyth Bridge ...... | | 9 23 | .... | 12 6 | | | 2 53 | 5 33 | 8 11 | 1010 | 2 22 | 6 50 |
| 5 6 | 4 6 | 2 9 | Longton .......... | | 9 31 | 9 54 | 1214 | | | 3 1 | 5 42 | 8 19 | 1018 | 2 30 | 6 58 |
| 5 10 | 4 5 | 2 11 | Stoke 160, 159 arr | | 9 38 | 10 0 | 1221 | | | 3 7 | 5 49 | 8 26 | 1025 | 2 40 | 7 5 |
| | | | To Newcstle, 162 dep | 7 15 | 9 50 | 10 3 | 1225 | | | 3 12 | 5 55 | 8 31 | 1030 | 2 45 | 7 15 |
| 6 0 | 4 7 | 3 0½ | Etruria .......... | 7 20 | 9 55 | .... | .... | | | .... | 6 0 | .... | 1035 | 2 50 | |
| 6 4 | 4 9 | 3 2 | Burslem (Longport) | 7 25 | 10 0 | 1010 | 1232 | | | 3 19 | 6 5 | 8 38 | 1040 | 2 56 | |
| 6 7 | 5 11 | 3 3 | Tunstall ....(castle) | 7 30 | .... | .... | .... | | | .... | 6 10 | .... | 1046 | 3 1 | |
| 6 10 | 5 2 | 3 5 | Kidsgrove J. (Hare- | 7 36 | 10 8 | 1018 | 1241 | | | 3 27 | 6 15 | 8 46 | 1052 | 3 7 | |
| 7 3 | 5 6 | 3 7½ | Alsager .......... | 7 42 | 1024 | 1024 | 1246 | | | 3 33 | 6 21 | 8 52 | 1059 | 3 14 | |
| 7 6 | 5 8 | 3 9 | Radway G [152,4,127 | 7 48 | .... | .... | .... | | | k | 6 26 | .... | 11 5 | 3 20 | |
| 8 4 | 6 4 | 4 2 | Crewe 113, 116, 151 | 8 0 | 1034 | 1034 | 1257 | | | 3 48 | 6 35 | 9 3 | 1115 | 3 30 | |
| .... | .... | .... | 152 CHESTER...... arr | 9 15 | 1158 | 1158 | 2 30 | .... | | 4 40 | 7 58 | 10 5 | 1150 | 4 50 | |
| .... | .... | .... | 113 L'POOL (Lm. St.) ,, | 9 45 | 1150 | 1150 | 2 30 | .... | | 5 35 | 8 0 | 1015 | 5 0 | 5 0 | |
| .... | .... | .... | 151 M'CHESTER (L.R.) ,, | 9 15 | 1145 | 1145 | 2 0 | .... | | 5 10 | 7 45 | 10 0 | 5 35 | 5 35 | 9 30 |
| 3 2 | 2 4 | 1 6½ | Uttoxeter (Dove Bnk.) | Stop | 9 5 | | 1148 | 1147 | | 2 33 | 5 14 | 7 50 | 9 58 | | 6 23 |
| 3 10 | 2 10 | 1 10½ | Rocester Junction..... | | 9 14 | | 1156 | [illegible] | | 2 43 | 5 23 | 8 0 | .. | | 6 32 |
| .... | .... | .... | Ashb'rn Branch. Rocester J. d | | 9 20 | | 1230 | 1230 | | 2 45 | 5 29 | 8 5 | 1026 | | 6 35 |
| .... | .... | .... | Norbury .. | | 9 27 | | 1236 | 1236 | | 2 51 | 5 35 | 8 11 | 1033 | | 6 42 |
| .... | .... | .... | Clifton .... | | 9 35 | | 1243 | 1243 | | 2 58 | 5 42 | 8 18 | 1041 | | 6 49 |
| .... | .... | .... | Ashborne a (All 123 class.) | | 9 40 | | 1248 | 1248 | | 3 2 | 5 45 | 8 22 | 1046 | | 6 55 |
| 4 5 | 3 3 | 2 2 | Alton .......... | | 9 22 | | 12 4 | | | | 5 31 | | | | 6 40 |
| 4 8 | 3 6 | 2 3½ | Oakamoor .......... | | 9 27 | | 12 9 | | | | 5 36 | | | | 6 45 |
| 5 1 | 3 10 | 2 6½ | Froghall .......... | 1&2 | 9 34 | | 1216 | | 4 10 | | 5 43 | | | | 6 52 |
| 5 10 | 4 5 | 2 10½ | Cheddleton .......... | mrn | 9 43 | | 1225 | | 4 18 | | 5 53 | | | | 7 1 |
| 6 3 | 4 8 | 3 1 | Leek 159.......... | 8 15 | 9 50 | | 1232 | | 4 25 | | 6 0 | | | | 7 8 |
| 6 7 | 4 11 | 3 3 | Rudyard or Horton.... | 8 21 | 9 56 | | 1238 | | .... | | 6 6 | | | | 7 14 |
| 7 1 | 5 3 | 3 6 | Rushton.......... | 8 28 | 10 3 | | 1245 | | .... | | 6 14 | | | | 7 21 |
| 7 5 | 5 6 | 3 8 | Bosley .......... | 8 34 | 10 9 | | 1251 | | .... | | 6 20 | | | | 7 27 |
| 7 8 | 5 9 | 3 10 | North Rode Junction.. | 8 40 | 1015 | | 1256 | | .... | | 6 25 | | | | 7 33 |
| 8 6 | 6 4 | 4 2½ | Macclesfield 150, 202 | 8 50 | 1025 | | 1 6 | | .... | | 6 35 | | | | 7 43 |
| 10 6 | 7 8 | 4 10½ | 150 M'CHESTR (L.R.) ar | 9 45 | 1115 | | 1 40 | | .... | | 7 35 | | | | 9 5 |

Uttoxeter, Stoke, and Crewe.

i Run through from Derby to Liverpool.

Tues. & Fri. only.

c 1&2 class only between Uttoxeter and Crewe.

1,2,3 class.

e 3rd class to Liverpool.

j 3rd class from Burton to Tutbury.

Wednesdays only.

a Run through from Derby to Manchester.

k Stops when required.

h 3rd class from Derby and Burton to Stockport and Manchester, via Macclesfield.

b 3rd class from Leicester to M'chester.

Stops at Fenton.

g 3rd class to Liverpool and Manchester, via Crewe.

Via Macclesfield see table below.

December 1870

## BURTON-ON-TRENT and TUTBURY.

| Miles | Down. | Week Days. | | | | | | | | | | | | | | | | Sundays. | | | |
|---|---|---|---|---|---|---|---|---|---|---|---|---|---|---|---|---|---|---|---|---|---|
| | Station Street, | mrn | mrn | mrn | | mrn | mrn | mrn S | | aft | aft | aft | aft | | aft | aft W | aft S | mrn | aft | aft | aft |
| — | Burton-on-Trent..........dep. | 7 10 | 8 0 | .... | .... | 9 9 | 1030 | 1150 | .... | 1 30 | 2 30 | 4 35 | 5 25 | .... | 7 5 | 9 5 | 1013 | 9 5 | 1 55 | 5 50 | 8 25 |
| 1 | Horninglow.................... | 7 13 | 8 3 | 8 30 | .... | 9 12 | 1033 | 1153 | .... | 1 33 | 2 33 | 4 38 | 5 28 | .... | 7 8 | 9 8 | 1016 | 9 8 | 1 58 | 5 53 | 8 28 |
| 2 | Stretton and Claymills ......... | 7 16 | 8 6 | 8 32 | .... | 9 15 | 1036 | .... | .... | 1 36 | 2 36 | 4 41 | 5 31 | .... | 7 11 | 9 11 | 1019 | .... | .... | 5 59 | 8 31 |
| 3 | Rolleston-on-Dove ............. | 7 19 | 8 9 | 8 35 | .... | 9 18 | 1039 | 1157 | .... | 1 39 | 2 39 | 4 44 | 5 34 | .... | 7 14 | 9 14 | 1022 | .... | .... | 6 2 | 8 34 |
| 5½ | Tutbury 626, 628..........arr. | 7 25 | 8 15 | 8 44 | .... | 9 24 | 1045 | 12 3 | .... | 1 45 | 2 45 | 4 50 | 5 40 | .... | 7 20 | 9 20 | 1028 | 9 20 | 2 8 | 6 8 | 8 40 |

| Miles | Up. | Week Days. | | | | | | | | | | | | | | | | Sundays. | | | |
|---|---|---|---|---|---|---|---|---|---|---|---|---|---|---|---|---|---|---|---|---|---|
| | | mrn | mrn | mrn | mrn | non S | | aft | aft | aft | aft | aft E | aft S | aft | aft S | aft F | aft S | mrn | | aft | aft |
| — | Tutbury........................dep. | 7 30 | 8 25 | 9 8 | 10 7 | 12 0 | .... | 1 3 | 2 2 | 3 2 | 4 56 | 5 48 | 5 55 | 8 25 | 9 25 | 9 45 | 1030 | 1148 | .... | 7 45 | 9 45 |
| 2¼ | Rolleston-on-Dove ............... | 7 34 | 8 29 | 9 12 | 1011 | 12 4 | .... | 1 7 | 2 6 | 3 6 | 5 0 | 5 52 | 5 59 | 8 29 | 9 29 | 9 49 | 1034 | .... | .... | 7 49 | 9 49 |
| 3½ | Stretton and Claymills ......... | 7 37 | 8 32 | .... | 1015 | 12 7 | .... | 1 10 | 2 9 | 3 9 | 5 3 | 5 55 | 6 2 | 8 32 | .... | 9 52 | 1037 | .... | .... | 7 52 | 9 52 |
| 4½ | Horninglow ............... [686 | 7 41 | 8 36 | 9 17 | 1018 | 1211 | .... | 1 14 | 2 13 | 3 13 | 5 7 | 5 59 | 6 6 | 8 36 | 9 34 | 9 56 | 1041 | 1156 | .... | 7 56 | 9 56 |
| 5½ | Burton-on-Trent A 483, 656 arr | 7 45 | 8 40 | 9 27 | 1024 | 1218 | .... | 1 18 | 2 17 | 3 17 | 5 11 | 6 3 | 6 10 | 8 40 | 9 40 | 10 5 | 1045 | 12 0 | .... | 8 0 | 10 5 |

A Station Street. E Except Saturdays. F Wednesdays only. S Saturdays only.
W Wednesdays and Saturdays.

July 1927

## UTTOXETER, CHEADLE, LONGTON, STOKE-ON-TRENT, HANLEY, and CONGLETON.

**Down.** — Week Days

| Miles | HOUR | 5 | B 6 | B 6 | 6 | B 6 | 7 | 7 | 7 | S 7 | | E 8 | S 8 | 8 | 8 | 8 | 9 | 9 | E 9 | S 10 | 9 | S 10 | E 10 | S 10 | S 11 | E 10 |
|---|---|---|---|---|---|---|---|---|---|---|---|---|---|---|---|---|---|---|---|---|---|---|---|---|---|---|
| — | Uttoxeter ...dep. | . | . | . | . | . | 0 | . | | 55 | . | . | . | 10 | . | . | . | . | . | . | 46 | . | . | . | . | . |
| 6 | Leigh ... | . | . | . | . | . | 10 | . | | H | . | . | . | 20 | . | . | . | . | . | . | . | . | . | . | . | . |
| — | Cheadle ...dep | . | . | . | . | . | . | . | 7S55 | . | . | 10 | . | . | . | . | . | . | . | . | . | . | . | . | . | . |
| — | Tean ... | . | . | . | . | . | . | . | 8S2 | . | . | 17 | . | . | . | . | . | . | . | . | . | . | . | . | . | . |
| 9¾ | Cresswell 527 ... | . | . | 5 | . | 55 | 16 | 45 | 8S5 | . | . | 20 | . | 26 | . | . | 8 | . | . | . | . | . | . | . | . | . |
| 11 | Blythe Bridge ... | 32 | . | 10 | 30 | **0** | 23 | 50 | 8 12 | . | . | 25 | 25 | 32 | . | 46 | 12 | 30 | . | . | . | 25 | 25 | 55 | . | 55 |
| 12¼ | Meir ... | 35 | . | 13 | 33 | 3 | 29 | 53 | 8 15 | . | . | 29 | 29 | 37 | . | 49 | 16 | 33 | . | . | . | 28 | 28 | 58 | . | 58 |
| 13¼ | Normacot ... | 37 | . | 15 | 35 | 5 | 30 | 55 | 8 17 | . | . | 31 | 31 | 39 | . | 51 | 18 | 35 | . | . | . | 30 | 30 | **0** | . | **0** |
| 14¼ | Longton ... | 40 | . | 18 | 38 | 8 | 33 | 58 | 8 20 | **24** | . | 34 | 34 | 42 | . | 54 | 21 | 38 | . | . | **7** | 33 | 33 | 3 | . | 3 |
| 15¼ | Fenton ... | 43 | . | 21 | 41 | 11 | 36 | **1** | 8 23 | . | . | 37 | 37 | . | . | 57 | 24 | 41 | . | . | . | 36 | 36 | 6 | . | 6 |
| 16½ | Stoke-on-Trent arr. | 47 | . | 25 | 45 | 15 | 40 | 6 | 8 27 | 32 | . | 41 | 41 | 48 | . | **1** | 29 | 46 | . | .. | 13 | 40 | 40 | 10 | . | 10 |
| | 528 to 534, 572 dep. | 50 | 5 | 30 | 51 | 20 | 42 | 10 | 8 33 | . | . | 44 | 44 | . | 54 | . | 35 | 54 | 57 | 1 | . | 43 | 43 | . | 23 | 23 |
| 17¾ | Etruria ... | 52 | 7 | 32 | 53 | 22 | 46 | 14 | 8 36 | . | . | 46 | 46 | . | 57 | . | 37 | 56 | **0** | 3 | . | 45 | 45 | . | 26 | 28 |
| 19 | Hanley ... | 53 | 13 | 38 | 58 | 27 | 51 | 18 | 8 42 | . | . | 52 | 52 | . | **2** | . | 44 | . | 4 | 9 | . | 50 | 50 | . | 30 | 30 |
| 19½ | Waterloo Road ... | . | . | . | . | 29 | 54 | 20 | 8 43 | . | . | . | . | . | 3 | . | 45 | . | . | . | . | . | . | . | 32 | 32 |
| 20 | Cobridge ... | **0** | . | 40 | **1** | 31 | 56 | 22 | 8 45 | . | . | 54 | 54 | . | 5 | . | 47 | . | 7 | 11 | . | 53 | 53 | . | 34 | 34 |
| 20¾ | Burslem ... | 3 | 16 | 43 | 4 | 34 | 59 | 25 | 8 48 | . | . | 57 | 57 | . | 8 | . | 50 | . | 10 | 14 | . | 56 | 56 | . | 37 | 37 |
| 21½ | Tunstall ... | 6 | 19 | 46 | 8 | 37 | **2** | 28 | 8 52 | . | . | **0** | **0** | . | 11 | . | 54 | . | 13 | 17 | . | 59 | 59 | . | 40 | 40 |
| 22 | Pitts Hill ... | 9 | . | 49 | 12 | 39 | . | 33 | 8 55 | . | . | 3 | 3 | . | 14 | . | . | . | . | . | . | . | **2** | . | 43 | . |
| 23 | Newchapel & Goldenhill ... | 13 | . | 55 | 17 | 43 | 6 | 37 | 8 58 | . | . | 7 | 7 | . | 18 | . | . | . | . | . | . | . | 4 | . | 46 | . |
| — | Kidsgrove Halt **A** ... | . | . | **0** | . | . | . | . | . | . | . | . | . | . | . | . | . | . | . | . | . | . | . | . | . | . |
| 25 | Kidsgrove ... | . | 27 | 4 | 22 | 49 | 11 | . | 9 4 | . | . | 13 | 13 | . | . | . | . | . | . | . | . | . | 11 | . | 52 | . |
| 27½ | Mow Cop & Scholar Green | . | 32 | 9 | . | . | . | . | . | . | . | 18 | 18 | . | . | . | . | . | . | . | . | . | 16 | . | 57 | . |
| 30½ | Congleton 532 ...arr. | . | 39 | 16 | . | 59 | . | . | . | . | . | 25 | 25 | . | . | . | . | . | . | . | . | . | 22 | . | **4** | . |

| Miles | HOUR | 11 | 11 | C 11 B | S 11 B | S 11 | E 11 | S 11 | S 12 | E 12 | S 12 | E 12 | 12 | E 1 | S 1 | S 12 | S 1 | 1 | | 2 | 2 | 2 | S 3 B | E 3 B | 3 | 4 | 3 |
|---|---|---|---|---|---|---|---|---|---|---|---|---|---|---|---|---|---|---|---|---|---|---|---|---|---|---|---|
| — | Uttoxeter ...dep. | . | . | . | . | 33 | 33 | 45 | . | . | 19 | 19 | . | . | . | 57 | 10 | . | . | . | 19 | . | . | . | . | . | 41 |
| 6 | Leigh ... | . | . | . | . | . | 43 | **0** | . | . | . | . | . | . | . | . | 20 | . | . | . | . | . | . | . | . | . | 51 |
| — | Cheadle ...dep | . | . | . | . | . | . | . | . | . | . | . | . | . | . | . | . | S 31 | . | . | . | . | . | . | . | . | . |
| — | Tean ... | . | . | . | . | . | . | . | . | . | . | . | . | . | . | . | . | S 38 | . | . | . | . | . | . | . | . | . |
| 9¾ | Cresswell 527 ... | 20 | . | . | . | . | 49 | 7 | . | . | . | . | . | . | 0 | . | 26 | S 41 | . | S 5 | . | E 42 | . | . | . | . | 57 |
| 11 | Blythe Bridge ... | 24 | . | . | 40 | . | 54 | 15 | . | 15 | 35 | 35 | 42 | 5 | 5 | **13** | 31 | 47 | . | 10 | 36 | 46 | . | . | 22 | . | **3** |
| 12¼ | Meir ... | 28 | . | . | 43 | . | . | 18 | . | 18 | . | . | 45 | 8 | 8 | . | 35 | 50 | . | 13 | . | 50 | . | . | 25 | . | 7 |
| 13¼ | Normacot ... | 31 | . | . | . | . | . | 20 | . | 20 | . | . | 47 | 10 | 10 | . | . | 52 | . | 15 | . | 52 | . | . | 27 | . | 9 |
| 14¼ | Longton ... | 33 | . | . | 47 | 52 | **1** | 23 | . | 23 | 42 | 42 | 50 | 13 | 13 | 20 | 39 | 55 | . | 18 | 43 | 55 | . | . | 30 | . | 12 |
| 15¼ | Fenton ... | 36 | . | . | . | . | . | 26 | . | 26 | . | . | 53 | 16 | 16 | . | . | 58 | . | 21 | . | 58 | . | . | 33 | . | 15 |
| 16½ | Stoke-on-Trent arr. | 40 | . | . | 53 | 59 | 7 | 30 | . | 30 | 51 | 48 | 58 | 20 | 20 | 27 | 45 | **2** | . | 25 | 49 | **2** | . | . | 37 | . | 19 |
| | 528 to 534, 572 dep. | . | 42 | 57 | 57 | **5** | 9 | . | 33 | 37 | . | 53 | **0** | 30 | 30 | . | 50 | 6 | . | 28 | 54 | E 5 | 10 | 20 | 40 | 10 | 25 |
| 17¾ | Etruria ... | . | 45 | **0** | **0** | 7 | 13 | . | 37 | 40 | . | 58 | 2 | 32 | 37 | . | 52 | 9 | . | 30 | 56 | E 7 | 12 | . | 43 | 12 | 27 |
| 19 | Hanley ... | . | 50 | 5 | 5 | . | . | . | 45 | 45 | . | . | 7 | 38 | 41 | . | . | 14 | . | 36 | . | E 13 | 18 | 27 | 48 | 18 | . |
| 19½ | Waterloo Road ... | . | 51 | . | . | . | . | . | 46 | 47 | . | . | . | 39 | 43 | . | . | 15 | . | 37 | . | . | . | . | . | 21 | . |
| 20 | Cobridge ... | . | 53 | . | . | . | . | . | 49 | 49 | . | . | 10 | 41 | 45 | . | . | 17 | . | 39 | . | E 15 | 20 | . | 51 | 23 | . |
| 20¾ | Burslem ... | . | 56 | 8 | 8 | . | . | . | 51 | 52 | . | . | 13 | 44 | 48 | . | . | 20 | . | 42 | . | E 18 | 23 | 30 | 54 | 26 | . |
| 21½ | Tunstall ... | . | 59 | 11 | 11 | . | . | . | 54 | 55 | . | . | 16 | 47 | 51 | . | . | 23 | . | 45 | . | E 21 | 26 | 33 | 57 | 29 | . |
| 22 | Pitts Hill ... | . | **3** | 14 | 14 | . | . | . | 57 | 58 | . | . | 19 | 50 | 54 | . | . | . | . | 48 | . | . | 29 | . | **0** | 42 | . |
| 23 | Newchapel & Goldenhill ... | . | 6 | 17 | 17 | . | . | . | **0** | **2** | . | . | 23 | 53 | 57 | . | . | . | . | 51 | . | . | 32 | . | 4 | 35 | . |
| — | Kidsgrove Halt **A** ... | . | . | . | . | . | . | . | 4 | . | . | . | . | 57 | **1** | . | . | . | . | . | . | . | . | . | . | 39 | . |
| 25 | Kidsgrove ... | . | . | 22 | 22 | . | . | . | 7 | . | . | . | . | **4** | 4 | . | . | . | . | 56 | . | . | 39 | 41 | . | 43 | . |
| 27½ | Mow Cop & Scholar Green | . | . | 27 | 27 | . | . | . | 12 | . | . | . | . | 9 | 9 | . | . | . | . | **1** | . | . | 44 | 46 | . | . | . |
| 30½ | Congleton 532 ...arr. | . | . | 34 | 34 | . | . | . | 19 | . | . | . | . | 16 | 16 | . | . | . | . | 8 | . | . | 51 | 53 | . | . | . |

Week Days—*Continued*

| HOUR | 4 | 4 | E 4 | 5 | 5 | E 5 | 5 | 5 | | 6 | 5 | 6 | F 6 | 6 | 7 | 7 | S 8 |
|---|---|---|---|---|---|---|---|---|---|---|---|---|---|---|---|---|---|
| Uttoxeter ...dep. | . | . | 20 | . | . | . | S 10 | 35 | . | . | 55 | . | . | 41 | . | . | . |
| Leigh ... | . | . | 32 | . | . | . | S 20 | . | . | . | **5** | . | . | . | . | . | . |
| Cheadle ...dep. | . | S 10 | . | . | . | 5 | . | . | . | . | . | . | . | . | . | . | . |
| Tean ... | . | S 17 | . | . | . | 12 | . | . | . | . | . | . | . | . | . | . | . |
| Cresswell 527 ... | . | S 25 | 41 | . | . | 16 | 30 | . | . | 0 | 12 | . | 46 | . | . | . | . |
| Blythe Bridge ... | . | 31 | 47 | . | 13 | . | 35 | 52 | . | 5 | 20 | . | 50 | **0** | . | 22 | . |
| Meir ... | . | 35 | 50 | . | 16 | . | 38 | . | . | 8 | 23 | . | 54 | . | . | 25 | |
| Normacot ... | . | 37 | 53 | . | 18 | . | 40 | . | . | 10 | 25 | . | 56 | | . | 27 | . |
| Longton ... | . | 41 | 56 | . | 21 | . | 43 | 59 | . | 13 | 28 | . | 59 | 6 | . | 30 | . |
| Fenton ... | . | 44 | 59 | . | 24 | . | 46 | . | . | 16 | 31 | . | **2** | 9 | . | 33 | . |
| Stoke-on-Trent arr. | . | 48 | **4** | . | 28 | . | 50 | **6** | . | 20 | 37 | . | 6 | 13 | . | 37 | . |
| 528 to 534, 572 dep. | 30 | 50 | . | 7 | 32 | . | 57 | 13 | . | 23 | . | 42 | 9 | 20 | 25 | 40 | 0 |
| Etruria ... | 32 | 54 | . | 10 | 34 | . | 59 | 15 | . | 26 | . | 44 | 11 | 24 | 27 | 42 | 2 |
| Hanley ... | 47 | **0** | . | 15 | 40 | . | **5** | . | . | 31 | . | 50 | 16 | . | 32 | 48 | 7 |
| Waterloo Road ... | . | 1 | . | 16 | . | . | 6 | . | . | . | . | 51 | . | . | . | . | . |
| Cobridge ... | 40 | 3 | . | 18 | 42 | . | 8 | . | . | 34 | . | 53 | 19 | . | 36 | 50 | 10 |
| Burslem ... | 43 | 6 | . | 21 | 45 | . | 11 | . | . | 37 | . | 56 | 22 | . | 40 | 53 | 13 |
| Tunstall ... | 46 | 9 | . | 24 | 49 | . | 14 | . | . | 40 | . | 59 | 25 | . | 42 | 56 | 16 |
| Pitts Hill ... | S 48 | 12 | . | 27 | 52 | . | 17 | . | . | 43 | . | S **2** | 28 | . | S 45 | 59 | 19 |
| Newchapel & Goldenhill ... | S 53 | 15 | . | 30 | 55 | . | 20 | . | . | 46 | . | S 6 | 31 | . | S 49 | **2** | 23 |
| Kidsgrove Halt **A** ... | . | 19 | . | 34 | 59 | . | 24 | . | . | 50 | . | . | 35 | . | . | 6 | . |
| Kidsgrove ... | . | 21 | . | 36 | **1** | . | 27 | . | . | 52 | . | . | 38 | . | . | 8 | . |
| Mow Cop & Scholar Green | . | 26 | . | . | E 8 | . | 32 | . | . | 58 | . | . | 42 | . | . | 13 | . |
| Congleton 532 ...arr. | . | 33 | . | . | E 15 | . | 39 | . | . | **5** | . | . | 49 | . | . | 20 | . |

| HOUR | S 7 | 8 | 8 | S 8 | E 9 | 9 | F 9 | S 9 | E 9 | 9 | 10 | S 9 | 10 | 10 | S 10 | 11 |
|---|---|---|---|---|---|---|---|---|---|---|---|---|---|---|---|---|
| Uttoxeter ...dep. | . | . | 5 | . | . | . | . | 10 | . | . | . | 56 | . | . | . | . |
| Leigh ... | . | . | 15 | . | . | . | . | 21 | . | . | . | **6** | . | . | . | . |
| Cheadle ...dep. | . | . | . | . | . | . | . | . | . | S 48 | . | . | . | . | . | . |
| Tean ... | . | . | . | . | . | . | . | . | . | S 55 | . | . | . | . | . | . |
| Cresswell 527 ... | . | . | 21 | . | . | S 5 | . | 30 | 30 | S **0** | . | 12 | . | . | . | . |
| Blythe Bridge ... | 55 | 17 | 26 | 47 | . | 10 | . | 35 | 35 | 5 | . | 17 | 35 | . | 55 | . |
| Meir ... | 58 | 20 | 30 | 50 | . | 13 | . | 38 | 38 | 8 | . | . | 38 | . | 58 | . |
| Normacot ... | **1** | 22 | . | 52 | . | 15 | . | 40 | 40 | 10 | . | . | 40 | . | . | . |
| Longton ... | 4 | 25 | 34 | 55 | . | 18 | . | 43 | 43 | 13 | . | 24 | 43 | . | **2** | . |
| Fenton ... | 7 | 28 | . | 58 | . | 21 | . | 46 | 46 | 16 | . | . | 46 | . | . | . |
| Stoke-on-Trent arr. | 15 | 34 | 40 | **2** | . | 25 | . | 50 | 50 | 20 | . | 30 | 50 | . | 8 | . |
| 528 to 534, 572 dep. | 20 | 42 | 48 | 5 | 5 | 30 | 35 | 53 | . | . | 23 | 32 | . | 53 | . | 10 |
| Etruria ... | 22 | 44 | 50 | 8 | 8 | 32 | 39 | 56 | . | . | 25 | 34 | . | 55 | . | 12 |
| Hanley ... | 28 | 50 | . | 13 | 13 | . | 45 | **0** | . | . | 30 | . | . | **0** | . | 18 |
| Waterloo Road ... | . | . | . | . | . | . | . | . | . | . | . | . | . | . | . | . |
| Cobridge ... | . | 52 | . | 15 | 15 | . | 47 | 3 | . | . | 33 | . | . | 3 | . | . |
| Burslem ... | 31 | 55 | . | 18 | 18 | . | 50 | 6 | . | . | 36 | . | . | 6 | . | 21 |
| Tunstall ... | 34 | 58 | . | 21 | 21 | . | 53 | 10 | . | . | 39 | . | . | 9 | . | 24 |
| Pitts Hill ... | 37 | **3** | . | 24 | 24 | . | 56 | 13 | . | . | 42 | . | . | 12 | . | . |
| Newchapel & Goldenhill ... | 40 | 8 | . | 27 | 28 | . | 59 | 16 | . | . | 45 | . | . | 15 | . | . |
| Kidsgrove Halt **A** ... | . | 12 | . | 31 | . | . | S **3** | 20 | . | . | 49 | . | . | 19 | . | . |
| Kidsgrove ... | 45 | 14 | . | 33 | . | . | 5 | 22 | . | . | 51 | . | . | 21 | . | . |
| Mow Cop & Scholar Green | 50 | 19 | . | 38 | . | . | 10 | . | . | . | S 56 | . | . | 26 | . | . |
| Congleton 532 ...arr. | 57 | 26 | . | 45 | . | . | 17 | . | . | . | S **3** | . | . | 33 | . | . |

Sundays

| HOUR | 9 | | 10 | 1 | 2 | 5 | 7 | 7 | | 8 | 9 | 10 | 10 | |
|---|---|---|---|---|---|---|---|---|---|---|---|---|---|---|
| Uttoxeter ...dep. | . | . | 56 | . | 46 | . | 11 | . | . | 57 | 31 | . | . | . |
| Leigh ... | . | . | **9** | . | . | . | 21 | . | . | . | 41 | . | . | . |
| Cheadle ...dep. | . | . | . | . | . | . | . | . | . | . | . | . | . | . |
| Tean ... | . | . | . | . | . | . | . | . | . | . | . | . | . | . |
| Cresswell 527 ... | . | . | 15 | . | . | . | 27 | . | . | . | 47 | . | . | . |
| Blythe Bridge ... | 32 | . | 20 | 45 | **3** | 55 | 32 | . | . | **14** | 52 | . | 35 | . |
| Meir ... | 36 | . | 25 | 48 | 8 | 58 | 37 | . | . | . | 56 | . | 39 | . |
| Normacot ... | . | . | 27 | . | . | . | 39 | . | . | . | 58 | . | 42 | . |
| Longton ... | 40 | . | 31 | 52 | 12 | **2** | 43 | . | . | 22 | **0** | . | 45 | . |
| Fenton ... | . | . | . | . | . | . | . | . | . | . | . | . | . | . |
| Stoke-on-Trent arr. | 46 | . | 37 | 58 | 18 | 8 | 50 | . | . | 29 | 7 | . | 52 | . |
| 528 to 534, 572 dep. | **0** | . | 48 | **13** | 22 | 25 | . | 53 | . | 45 | 12 | 15 | **5** | . |
| Etruria ... | 2 | . | 50 | 15 | 24 | 28 | . | 55 | . | 47 | 14 | 17 | 7 | . |
| Hanley ... | . | . | . | . | . | . | . | **0** | . | . | . | 22 | . | . |
| Waterloo Road ... | . | . | . | . | . | . | . | . | . | . | . | . | . | . |
| Cobridge ... | . | . | . | . | . | . | . | 3 | . | . | . | 25 | . | . |
| Burslem ... | . | . | . | . | . | . | . | 6 | . | . | . | 28 | . | . |
| Tunstall ... | . | . | . | . | . | . | . | 9 | . | . | . | 31 | . | . |
| Pitts Hill ... | . | . | . | . | . | . | . | . | . | . | . | . | . | . |
| Newchapel & Goldenhill ... | . | . | . | . | . | . | . | . | . | . | . | . | . | . |
| Kidsgrove Halt **A** ... | . | . | . | . | . | . | . | . | . | . | . | . | . | . |
| Kidsgrove ... | . | . | . | . | . | . | . | . | . | . | . | . | . | . |
| Mow Cop & Scholar Green | . | . | . | . | . | . | . | . | . | . | . | . | . | . |
| Congleton 532 ...arr. | . | . | . | . | . | . | . | . | . | . | . | . | . | . |

**A** Alighting platform only **B** Thro' Train to Manchester (L R), page 532 **C** Thurs only **E** Except Sats **F** Thro' Train to Manchester, except on Sats
**H** Stops to take up for beyond Crewe on notice at Station **S** or **S** Sats only

August 1933

## DERBY, UTTOXETER, and STAFFORD

| Miles | Down | Week Days only mrn | | aft E | aft S | aft | aft | |
|---|---|---|---|---|---|---|---|---|
| | Derby (Friargate) ...dep. | 9 20 | .. | 1 55 | 1 55 | 5 0 | 7 27 | .. |
| 2¼ | Mickleover, for Radburn ... | 9 26 | .. | 2 1 | 2 1 | 5 **6** | 7 34 | .. |
| 6¼ | Etwall ... | 9 33 | .. | 2 10 | 2 10 | 5 13 | 7 42 | .. |
| 7¾ | Egginton Junction ... arr. | 9 36 | .. | 2 13 | 2 13 | 5 16 | 7 45 | .. |
| | dep. | 9 39 | .. | 2 15 | 2 18 | 5 21 | 7 47 | .. |
| 10¾ | Tutbury ... | 9 46 | .. | 2H25 | 2H28 | 5K30 | 7 54 | .. |
| 14 | Sudbury ... | 9 52 | .. | 2H35 | 2H38 | 5 36 | 8 0 | .. |
| 15¼ | Marchington ... | 9 56 | .. | 2 39 | 2 42 | 5 40 | 8 4 | .. |
| 18½ | Uttoxeter 519, 526, 528, 572 arr. | 10 1 | .. | 2 44 | 2 47 | 5 45 | 8 9 | .. |
| | dep. | 10 5 | .. | 2 48 | 2 52 | 5 50 | 8 14 | .. |
| 23¼ | Grindley ... | 1017 | .. | 3 1 | 3H9 | 6 2 | 8 26 | .. |
| 25¼ | Chartley ... | 1022 | .. | 3 5 | 3 13 | 6 6 | 8 30 | .. |
| 27¼ | Ingestre **B** ... | 1033 | .. | 3H13 | 3H21 | 6 11 | 8 40 | .. |
| 29 | Salt ... | 1037 | .. | 3 17 | 3 26 | 6 15 | 8 44 | .. |
| 32 | Stafford (Common) ... | 1045 | .. | 3 26 | 3 38 | 6 22 | 8 51 | .. |
| 33¼ | " (Town) 478, 487 arr | 1049 | .. | 3 30 | 3 42 | 6 25 | 8 55 | .. |

| Miles | Up | Week Days only mrn | | aft | aft | | aft | |
|---|---|---|---|---|---|---|---|---|
| | Stafford (Town) ...dep. | 9 8 | .. | 2A10 | 4 38 | .. | 7 29 | .. |
| 1¼ | " (Common) ... | 9 9 | .. | 2A14 | 4 42 | .. | 7 36 | .. |
| 4¼ | Salt ... | 9 16 | .. | 2A21 | 4 49 | .. | 7 45 | .. |
| 6½ | Ingestre **B** ... | 9 24 | .. | 2A29 | 4 54 | .. | 7 51 | .. |
| 8 | Chartley ... | 9 29 | .. | 2A34 | 4 59 | .. | 7 56 | .. |
| 10¼ | Grindley ... | 9 36 | .. | 2J41 | 5 5 | .. | 8D11 | .. |
| 15¼ | Uttoxeter 519, 526, 528, 572 arr. | 9 47 | .. | 2J51 | 5 16 | .. | 8 21 | .. |
| | dep. | 9 49 | .. | 2 55 | 5 20 | .. | 8 24 | .. |
| 18½ | Marchington ... | 9 55 | .. | 3 1 | 5 26 | .. | 8 30 | .. |
| 20 | Sudbury ... | 10 0 | .. | 3 5 | 5 30 | .. | 8 34 | .. |
| 23¼ | Tutbury ... | 10 6 | .. | 3 12 | 5 36 | .. | 8 41 | .. |
| 26 | Egginton Junc 900 ... arr. | 1012 | .. | 3 18 | 5 42 | .. | 8 47 | .. |
| | dep. | 1013 | .. | 3 21 | 5 44 | .. | 8 51 | .. |
| 27½ | Etwall ... | 1017 | .. | .. | 5 48 | .. | 8 55 | .. |
| 31¼ | Mickleover, for Radburn ... | 1025 | .. | .. | 5 56 | .. | .. | .. |
| 33¾ | Derby (F) **C** 656, 702 arr. | 1030 | .. | 3 35 | 6 1 | .. | 9 4 | .. |

**A** 3 mins. later on Sats. **B** Under ¼ mile to Weston & Ingestre Sta. **C** Over 1 mile to L. M. & S. Sta **D** Arr. 8 1 aft.
**E** Except Sats. **H** Arr. 5 mins. *earlier*. **J** 2 mins. later on Sats. **K** Arr. 5 26 aft. **S** Sats. only

March 1938

**Table 132**

## BURTON-ON-TRENT and TUTBURY

| Miles | | Week Days a.m | a.m | | a.m | | a.m S | | a.m E | | p.m | | p.m | | p.m | | p.m | | Sundays p.m | | p.m | |
|---|---|---|---|---|---|---|---|---|---|---|---|---|---|---|---|---|---|---|---|---|---|---|
| — | Burton-on-Trent ...... dep | 7 15 | 8 0 | .. | 9 8 | .. | 1040 | .. | 1110 | .. | 1 33 | .. | 4 30 | .. | 5 13 | .. | 8 12 | .. | 2 5 | .. | 5 28 | .. |
| 5¼ | Tutbury ... arr | 7 25 | 8 10 | .. | 9 18 | .. | 1050 | .. | 1120 | .. | 1 43 | .. | 4 40 | .. | 5 23 | .. | 8 22 | .. | 2 17 | .. | 5 40 | .. |

| Miles | | Week Days am | | a.m | | a.m | | p.m | | p.m | | p.m | | p.m | | p.m | | | Sundays p.m | | p.m | |
|---|---|---|---|---|---|---|---|---|---|---|---|---|---|---|---|---|---|---|---|---|---|---|
| — | Tutbury ... dep | 7 32 | .. | 8 40 | .. | 10 0 | .. | 1 5 | .. | 3 8 | .. | 4 45 | .. | 5 35 | .. | 8 37 | .. | .. | 4 15 | .. | 7 15 | .. |
| 5¼ | Burton-on-Trent ...... arr | 7 42 | .. | 8 50 | .. | 1010 | .. | 1 15 | .. | 3 18 | .. | 4 55 | .. | 5 47 | .. | 8 47 | .. | .. | 4 27 | .. | 7 28 | .. |

**E** Except Saturdays
**S** Saturdays only

May 1956

# 1. Derby to Stoke-on-Trent

## DERBY

## DERBY

**Chaddesden Sidings**

**Midland Works**
(Locomotive)

II. The 1938 edition is scaled at 6ins to 1 mile and it features most of the ex-MR works. Near the words "Towing Path", lower right, is the town's gas works. Its coal arrived by boat, but most of the coke left by rail. The main line to Burton runs to the lower border. The goods yards adjacent to it closed on 4th January 1965.

1.    The west elevation is seen in about 1920. Trams operated from 1904 to 1934 and trolleybuses ran until 1967. The building seen was completed in 1891, there having been two temporary structures until May 1840, when the first stone building appeared. The nearest tram will run to the nearest station on our route. (A.Dudman coll.)

2.    We move forward to 3rd June 1950 and find a long ladder standing under some of the faulty glazing. Class 2P no. 40499 has reached a dip in the platform, so that its wheels can be seen. The platforms were extensively rebuilt in 1952-54, along with their buildings. (H.C.Casserley)

3.   More dangerous glass is evident on 25th April 1953 as class 4P no. 40931 waits by Derby 'A' Box. This was in use from 1952 to 1969. The parcels van has a look-out for the guard on the left of the door. He could check the integrity of his train. (H.C.Casserley)

Temperance Society 1911

4.   It is September 1957 and all the building work was complete, but the signalling was yet to be modernised. The curiosity on the left was for the benefit of the lamp man. Platform lighting had gone from gas to electricity. Class 5 4-6-0 no. 73135 was bound for Crewe via Stoke-on-Trent. (M.J.Stretton coll.)

5.   Merry-go-round coal hoppers are hauled south on 16th September 1982 by no. 56003. They will also use our route via Uttoxeter. The station had the suffix MIDLAND from 25th September 1950 until 6th May 1968. It had been STATION STREET from 1867 to 1906. (T.Heavyside)

6.     Setting out from Derby on 23rd October 2014 is East Midlands Trains unit no. 156401 on the hourly service to Crewe. The station is crossed by a footbridge providing pedestrian access to the Pride Park development on former railway land, as well as between the concourse and platforms. This footbridge, which was built in 2001 with a financial contribution from Derby City Council, became the subject of complex negotiations once East Midlands Trains installed ticket barriers controlling access to the station. The ex-MR office block is on the right. The works had a staff of over 8000 by 1940. (P.D.Shannon)

**Other views can be seen in** *Tamworth to Derby***,** *Derby Tramways* **and** *Derby Trolleybuses***. The first contains extensive illustrations of the railway works.**

7.     The spacious facilities and smart presentation are seen on 10th October 2015, with no. 153308 bound for Crewe at 11.42. It would call at all stations via Uttoxeter, except Peartree. The train will soon pass the site of Ramsline Halt, which was on the west side of the line, from 20th January 1990. It was built for football supporters, but was only used three times. (V.Mitchell)

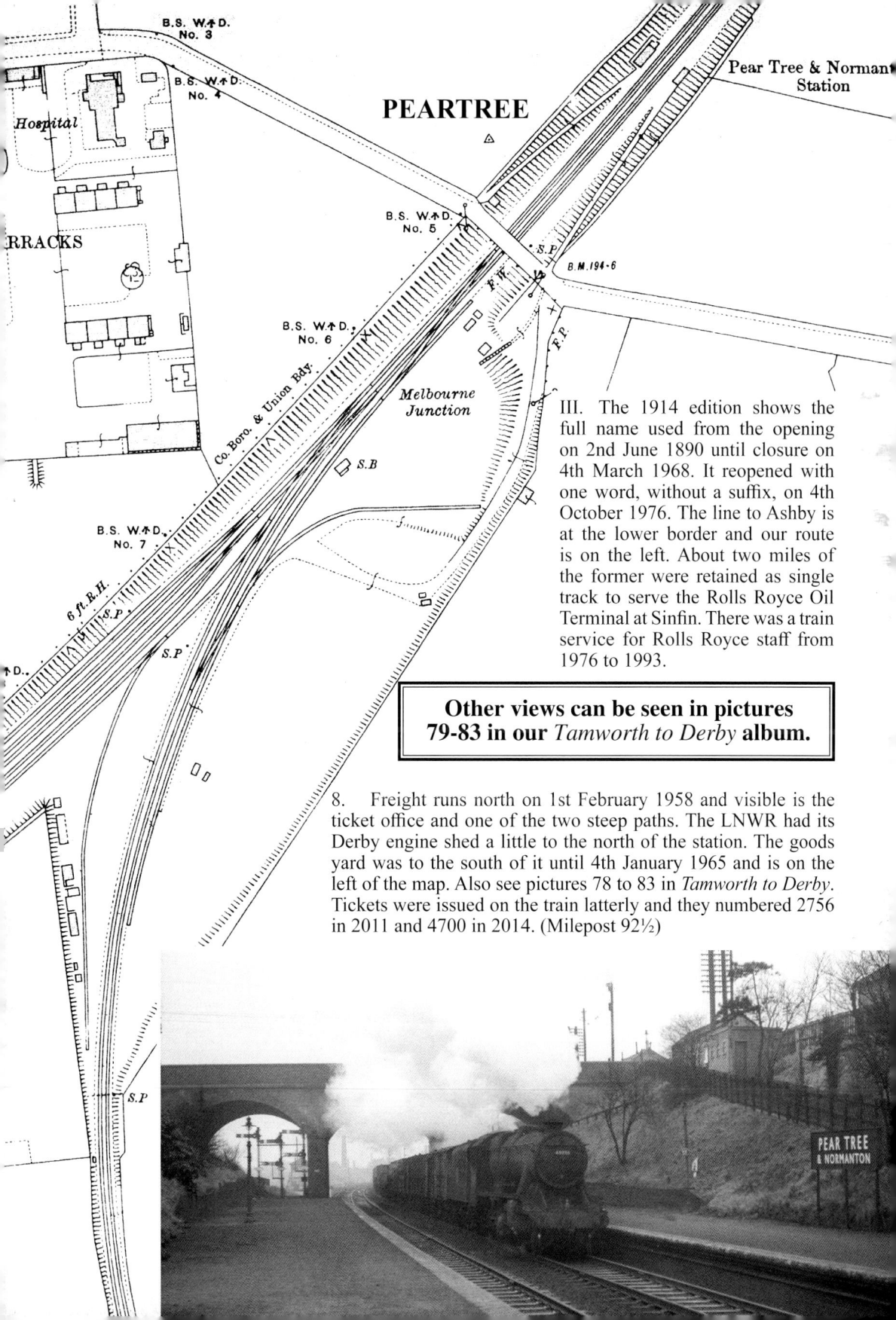

## PEARTREE

B.S. W✠D. No. 3

B.S. W✠D. No. 4

Hospital

RRACKS

B.S. W✠D. No. 5

B.S. W✠D. No. 6

B.S. W✠D. No. 7

6 ft.R.H.

S.P.

Co. Boro. & Union Bdy.

Melbourne Junction

S.B

S.P.

S.P.

Pear Tree & Norman Station

S.P.

B.M.194·6

F.P.

Pear Tree & Normant Station

III. The 1914 edition shows the full name used from the opening on 2nd June 1890 until closure on 4th March 1968. It reopened with one word, without a suffix, on 4th October 1976. The line to Ashby is at the lower border and our route is on the left. About two miles of the former were retained as single track to serve the Rolls Royce Oil Terminal at Sinfin. There was a train service for Rolls Royce staff from 1976 to 1993.

> **Other views can be seen in pictures 79-83 in our *Tamworth to Derby* album.**

8. Freight runs north on 1st February 1958 and visible is the ticket office and one of the two steep paths. The LNWR had its Derby engine shed a little to the north of the station. The goods yard was to the south of it until 4th January 1965 and is on the left of the map. Also see pictures 78 to 83 in *Tamworth to Derby*. Tickets were issued on the train latterly and they numbered 2756 in 2011 and 4700 in 2014. (Milepost 92½)

PEAR TREE & NORMANTON

9. Stenson Junction is where trains from Nottingham can join the main line from Derby to Burton, which is on the left. In the foreground of this 1977 panorama are the lines serving Willington Power Station, which were in use in 1959-99. They join the Loughborough route at the right border. It also serves trains bound for Nottingham. (J.Whitehouse)

10. For several years, Colas Rail held the contract to deliver aviation fuel from Grangemouth to the Rolls Royce works at Sinfin, Derby. Its weekly train was routed via the Uttoxeter line. No. 66850 has just cleared the points at North Staffordshire Junction with the 21.15 Grangemouth-Sinfin train on 24th July 2012. In the distance is the footbridge, which had recently replaced a pedestrian foot crossing at this location. On the left had been one of the signals that once regulated trains serving Willington Power Station. (P.D.Shannon)

# EGGINTON JUNCTION

11.   We look south in about 1920, as GNR class D2 4-4-0 no. 1380 waits on the GNR Derbyshire extension line with a train from Stafford to Derby Friar Gate. The village housed 412 in 1901 and 355 in 1961. A military depot, with sidings, was built west of the station in 1942 and it served the Central Vehicle Depot until 1989. The tracks were lifted in 1992. (RAS)

Issued by the **N.S.R.** Co. subject to the Company's regulations and to the conditions in their Time Tables. Not Transferable.
PARLIAMENTARY.
DERBY N.S. To
EGGINTON
AVAILABLE ON DAY OF ISSUE FOR ONE JOURNEY ONLY
EGGINTON 21          FARE 7½d
468

3rd-SINGLE   SINGLE-3rd
Derby                    Derby
  Derby        To
Crewe                    Crewe
      CREWE
    Via UTTOXETER
    Via Stoke
(M) 7/6 H       7/6 H (M)
ForConditions see over   ForConditions see over
2329                      2329

IV. The 1922 edition has our MR route from Derby on the right and the LNWR one at the top. This is blue on the back cover map. The first station had been about ¼ mile to the east from 1849 until 1st July 1878, when this one opened with the suffix JUNCTION. Its signal box was beyond the left border; its 47 levers had been reduced to 14 by 1972. The points went in 1968.

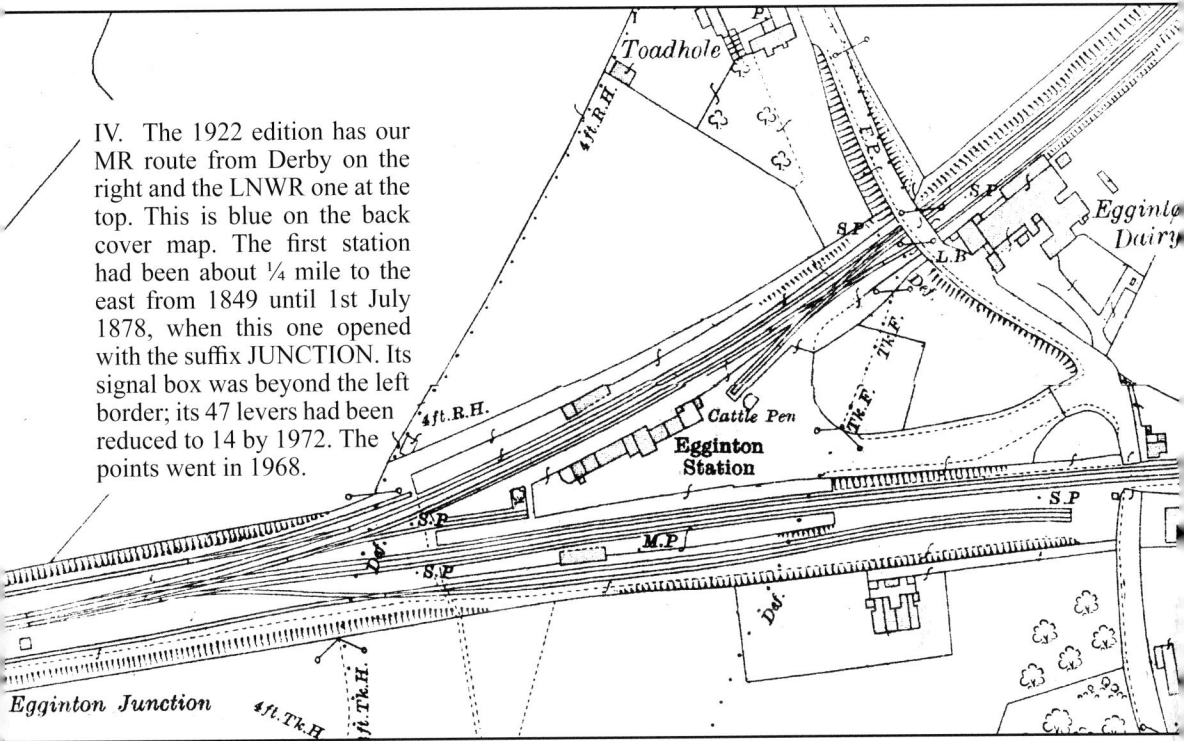

Toadhole

4 ft. R.H.

Egginto Dairy

L.B

S.P

Def.

Tk.F.

Tk.F.

Cattle Pen

Egginton Station

4 ft. R.H.

S.P

Def.

S.P

M.P.

Def.

S.P

Egginton Junction  4ft. Tk.H.  4ft. Tk.H.

12. This panorama was recorded from a signal post at the west end of the station in about 1950. On the left is the dairy chimney and on the right is the goods yard, which closed on 7th August 1961. Passenger service ceased on 5th March 1962, but the station house avoided demolition. The route was used by Summer seaside trains between Manchester/Liverpool and Cromer/Yarmouth, also between Derby/Nottingham and Rhyl/Llandudno. In the distance is Hilton Crossing. (W.A.Camwell/SLS)

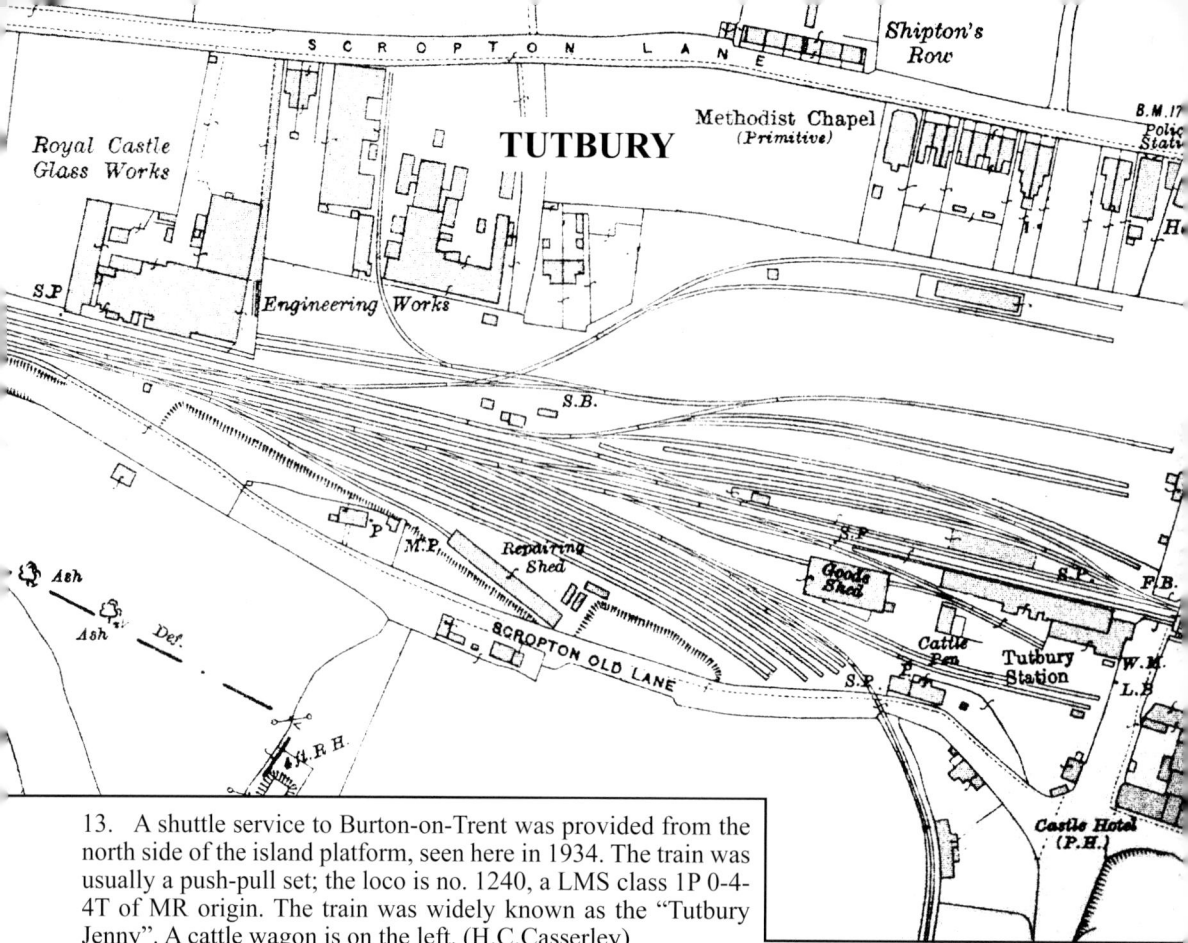

Map labels:
S C R O P T O N   L A N E

Shipton's Row

Methodist Chapel
(Primitive)

B.M.17
Polic
Stati

**TUTBURY**

Royal Castle
Glass Works

H.

S.P.

Engineering Works

S.B.

S.P.

Ash

Ash   Def.

P   M.P.   Repairing
Shed

S.P.

Goods
Shed

S.P.   F.B.

SCROPTON OLD LANE

Cattle
Pen   Tutbury
Station   W.M.
L.B.

S.P.

A.R.H.

Castle Hotel
(P.H.)

13. A shuttle service to Burton-on-Trent was provided from the north side of the island platform, seen here in 1934. The train was usually a push-pull set; the loco is no. 1240, a LMS class 1P 0-4-4T of MR origin. The train was widely known as the "Tutbury Jenny". A cattle wagon is on the left. (H.C.Casserley)

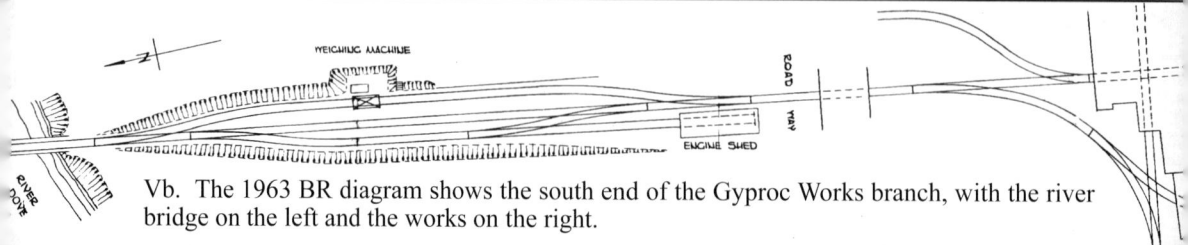

WEIGHING MACHINE

ROAD

WAY

ENGINE SHED

RIVER

Vb. The 1963 BR diagram shows the south end of the Gyproc Works branch, with the river bridge on the left and the works on the right.

Va. The 1922 edition has Yard Box in the centre of the left page. Its replacement in 1953 had 35 levers and closed on 22nd May 1983. Gate Box is at the join of the pages. The population was 1971 in 1901, rising to 2566 in 1961, but the station was in the smaller parish of Hatton. Tutbury Castle is marked on the next map. Of great antiquity, it attracts many visitors. Few gaze at the equally durable goods shed. On the right page is the private siding for the milk factory, which was opened by the Nestlé Anglo-Swiss Condensed Milk Company in 1901. At the bottom of the left page is the gate on the siding to Tutbury Mill. This produced cotton until 1888 and was water-powered. Henry Newton acquired it in 1890 for the manufacture of plaster. The necessary gypsum rock came from Fauld mine and was conveyed by the NSR from Scropton to the sidings on the left page. From here to the mill, from 1953, haulage was by J.C.Staton's Peckett 0-4-0ST no. 1666. A Yorkshire Engine Co. 0-6-0 diesel was used in the final few years until closure in 1983. The mill was closed in October 1968 and was demolished in 1972. However, gypsum was brought by road from Fauld and loaded here, for processing elsewhere. Tutbury Glass Works' coke requirements also came to these sidings until gas was used.

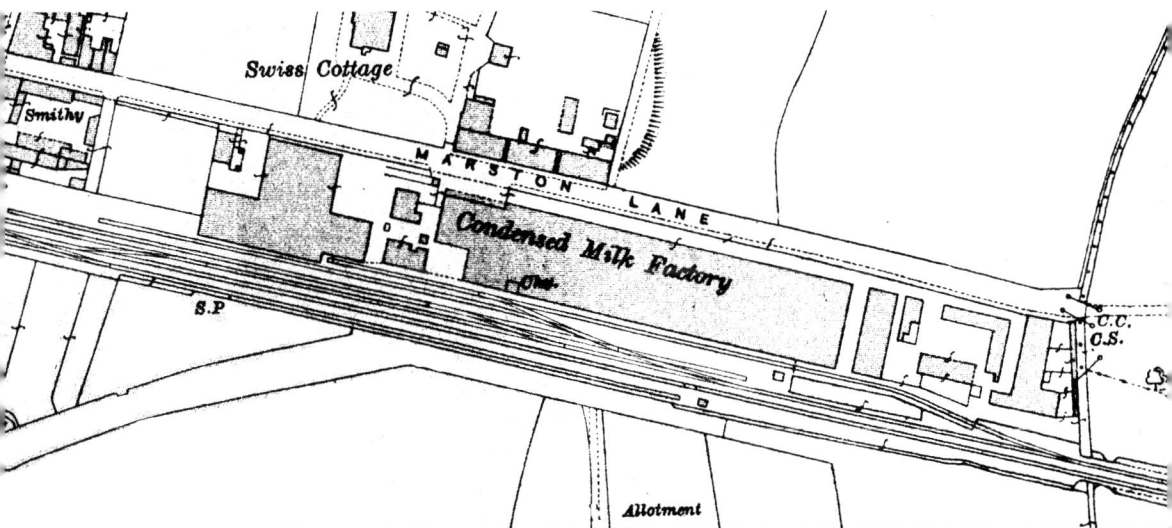

14. Although regular service south had ceased on 1st January 1949, BR class 2MT 2-6-2T no. 84008 departs for Burton, propelling its train and hauling one carriage on 31st July 1954. The roof of Crossing Box is beyond the footbridge. There were once five private sidings nearby. (J.P.Wilson/RAS)

15. Yard Box is in the distance as we look west from the footbridge on 25th May 1957. Class 4MT 2-6-4T no.42627 waits with a SLS Special. It ran from and back to Birmingham via Walsall, a mineral line to Rugeley, Stoke, Leek Brook, Caldon Quarry, Congleton, North Rode, Leek, Burton and Lichfield, all for 21s 6d. The goods yard closed on 6th July 1964; by 1938, it had a 10-ton crane. On the right is the milk dock, although the dairy had its own siding.
(R.J.Buckley/Initial Photographs)

16. The 13.20 Crewe to Derby DMU runs in on 7th December 1957, while class 2MT 2-6-2T no. 84007 waits with the 14.35 to Burton-on-Trent. The station closed to passengers on 7th November 1966, but reopened on 3rd April 1989, with new platforms, one each side of the level crossing. The suffix '& HATTON' was added at that time. Both platforms could take four coaches. (E.Wilmshurst)

17. Yard Box is nearest, on the left. Its 35-lever frame was in use from 20th December 1953 until 22nd May 1983. In the distance, in April 1983, is Crossing Box, which opened in about 1872 with 26 levers, but these were eventually reduced to nine. The barriers arrived in 1974. Gypsum arrived by road from Fauld for loading here, but the tonnage dropped steadily in the 1970s. In the background is the expanded dairy building, which was producing coffee, notably Nescafé from 1959. Passengers numbered 52,182 in 2010 and 63,430 in 2014. (N.Allsop)

**3rd · SINGLE**

**TUTBURY**
TO
**BURTON-ON-TRENT**

(M)

Fare 0/5½

FOR CONDITIONS SEE OVER

8107 CHILD   CHILD 8107

L.M.&S.R. For con-        L.M.&S.R. For con-
ditions see Back          ditions see Back
N.A.X.A.F. on LEAVE       N.A.X.A.F. on LEAVE
**THIRD CLASS**           **THIRD CLASS**
**SINGLE**                **SINGLE**
Tutbury                   Tutbury
            **Tutbury To**
**LONGPORT**
Longport                  Longport
2/10  Z      FARE      2/10  Z

437      437

# WEST OF TUTBURY

18.   New sidings were laid on the south side of the route in 1939 to serve the RAF Fauld underground bomb store created in a disused gypsum mine. The new signal box with 25 levers was usable until 15th August 1971. An internal two-foot gauge railway was laid and this evidence was obtained on 6th March 1981. Nearest is a Greenwood & Batley battery locomotive of 1942 and beyond it is a 48HP Ruston diesel, used for surface work. Over 10,000 tons of bombs were despatched each month in the Summer of 1944. (V.J.Bradley/A.Neale coll.)

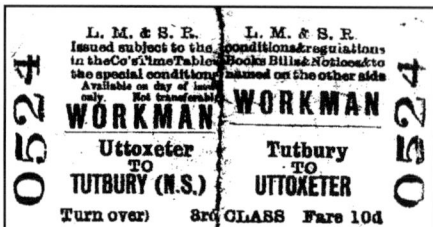

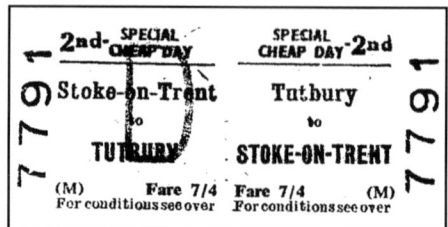

# SCROPTON

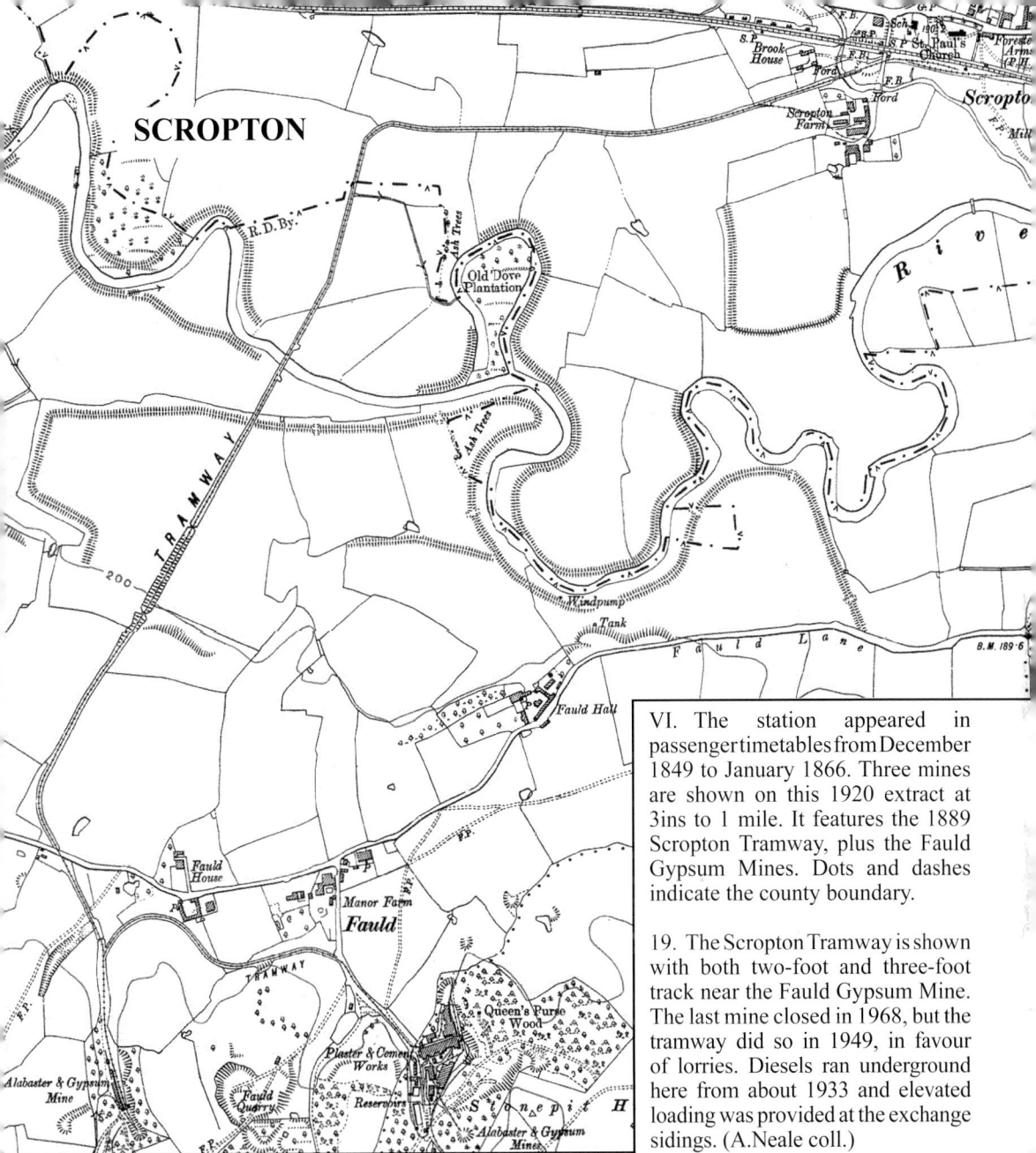

VI. The station appeared in passenger timetables from December 1849 to January 1866. Three mines are shown on this 1920 extract at 3ins to 1 mile. It features the 1889 Scropton Tramway, plus the Fauld Gypsum Mines. Dots and dashes indicate the county boundary.

19. The Scropton Tramway is shown with both two-foot and three-foot track near the Fauld Gypsum Mine. The last mine closed in 1968, but the tramway did so in 1949, in favour of lorries. Diesels ran underground here from about 1933 and elevated loading was provided at the exchange sidings. (A.Neale coll.)

20. Tutbury Plaster Work's fleet is seen on 27th August 1960. Two secondhand Peckett 0-4-0STs (1666 of 1924 and 2112 of 1949) worked the Plaster Works branch in the 1960s, until replaced by a diesel provided by an outside contractor. A new processing plant was completed at Fauld in 1952. (J.Hill/A.Neale coll.)

21. The remains of the exchange sidings are seen on 5th March 1966, with the signal box in the distance. The illusion of the left track being on the loop is due to its situation on the edge of a dock. (A.Neale coll.)

22. Passing on 29th March 1997 is ex-LNER class A2 4-6-2 no. 60532 *Blue Peter*, as it hauls an excursion running from Cleethorpes to Chester. The 23-lever frame in Scropton box was still in use nearly 20 years later. The church confirms the location on the map. The building on the right was once the narrow gauge engine shed, but was converted to a dwelling. (J.Whitehouse)

N.S.R. THIRD CLASS.
SUDBURY To
TUTBURY
AVAILABLE FOR ONE JOURNEY ON DAY OF ISSUE ONLY
Turn over    Tutbury 76    Fare 3d.
391

2nd-PRIVILEGE SINGLE    PRIVILEGE SINGLE -2nd
Sudbury (Staffs) To
Sudbury (Staffs)    Sudbury (Staffs)
Uttoxeter    Uttoxeter
UTTOXETER
(M)   0/4   Fare   0/4   (M)
For conditions see over   For conditions see over
2175      2175

# SUDBURY

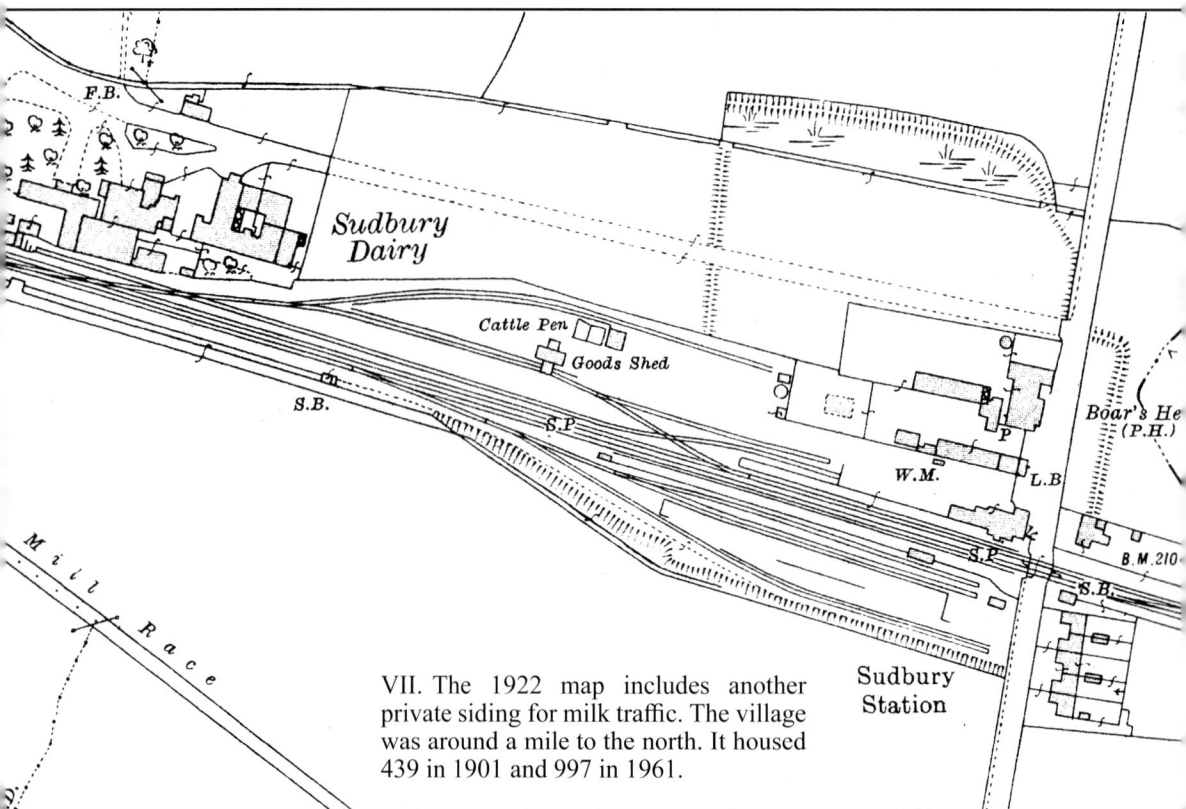

VII. The 1922 map includes another private siding for milk traffic. The village was around a mile to the north. It housed 439 in 1901 and 997 in 1961.

23. This is our first stop in Staffordshire and the team featured on this postcard includes shift workers and the track gang. Milk churns were often seen until the 1930s. (P.Laming coll.)

24.   It is 9th September 1961 and class 6P5F 2-6-0 no. 42856 is running west with mixed freight. It is passing over the A515, which received its number in 1919. (R.J.Buckley/Initial Photographics)

25.   A panorama from 12th April 1964 includes parts of both yards. Their traffic ceased on 3rd May 1965, whereas passengers were conveyed until 7th November 1966. The spots are insulators carrying wires to the lamps, which are not clear. Visible immediately beyond the signal at the end of the platform is the connection added in 1942 to the extensive MOD sidings on the down side of the line. All sidings were taken out of use in November 1970. (Bentley coll.)

26.   The NSR completed the 26-lever box, which is seen in 1964. It was still in use in 2016, but with only 14 levers. The gates were replaced by barriers in 1990. A smaller box with a ground frame with 10 levers was west of the platform until November 1970. (Bentley coll.)

**N.S. RY. LOCAL 6$^D$.**

Ticket for ONE BICYCLE, PERAMBULATOR, or MAIL CART, ACCOMPANIED BY PASSENGER. FOR A SINGLE JOURNEY ONLY.

**SUDBURY To**

Any North Stafford Station not exceeding

(12) **MILES** THEREFROM

For Conditions see back hereof.

590

N.S.R. PARLIAMENTARY.

**MARCHINGTON To**

**DERBY (G.N.)**

Via Eggington and Etwall

AVAILABLE FOR ONE JOURNEY ON DAY OF ISSUE ONLY

Turn over     Derby G.N. 50     Fare 1/4

4070

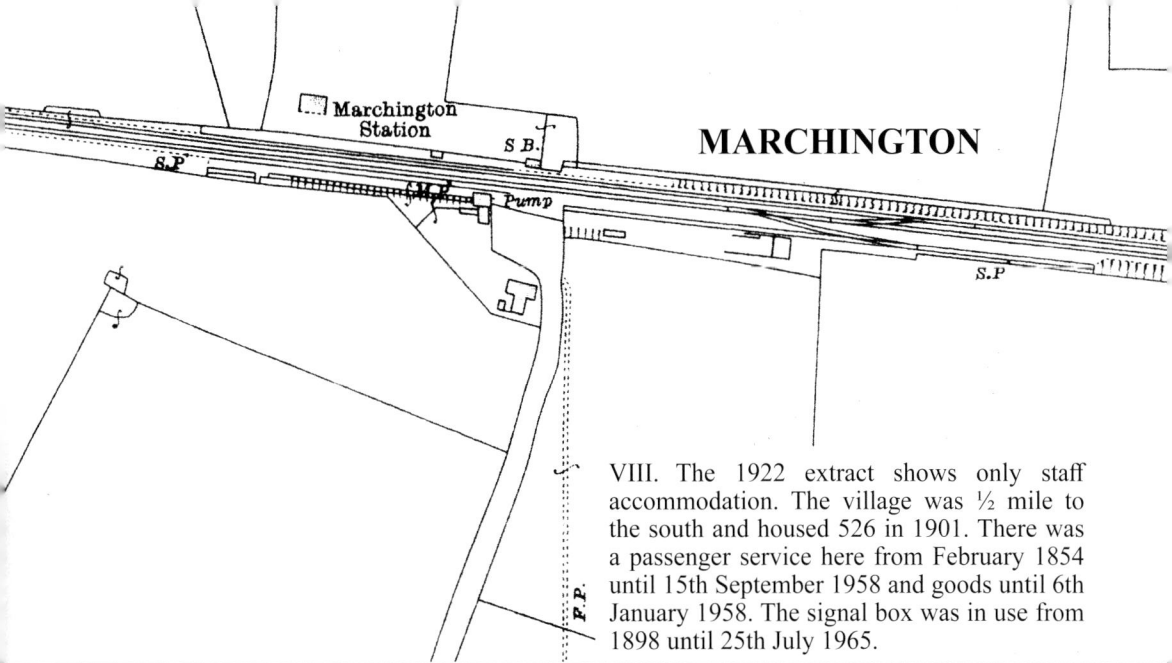

Marchington Station
S B.
S.P
LMR
Pump
S.P
P.P.

# MARCHINGTON

VIII. The 1922 extract shows only staff accommodation. The village was ½ mile to the south and housed 526 in 1901. There was a passenger service here from February 1854 until 15th September 1958 and goods until 6th January 1958. The signal box was in use from 1898 until 25th July 1965.

27.    We look east in the 1950s and ¾ mile away was Dovefields signal box, which had 25 levers and opened in 1942 to access sidings serving an American army depot on the north side of the line. It included a locomotive depot for three engines and had a daily train initially. The box closed on 20th August 1967. It has 12 levers. Parts of the platform edges were still visible in 2016. (W.A.Camwell/SLS)

# UTTOXETER

IX. The 1937 survey is at 20ins to 1 mile and we arrive at the top. Trains to Ashbourne and the Churnet Valley Line depart on the left. The lower part continues on the next map, but this includes one of the two cranes (C.), both of which were rated at 5-tons capacity. The town grew from 6232 in 1901 to 13,089 in 2011.

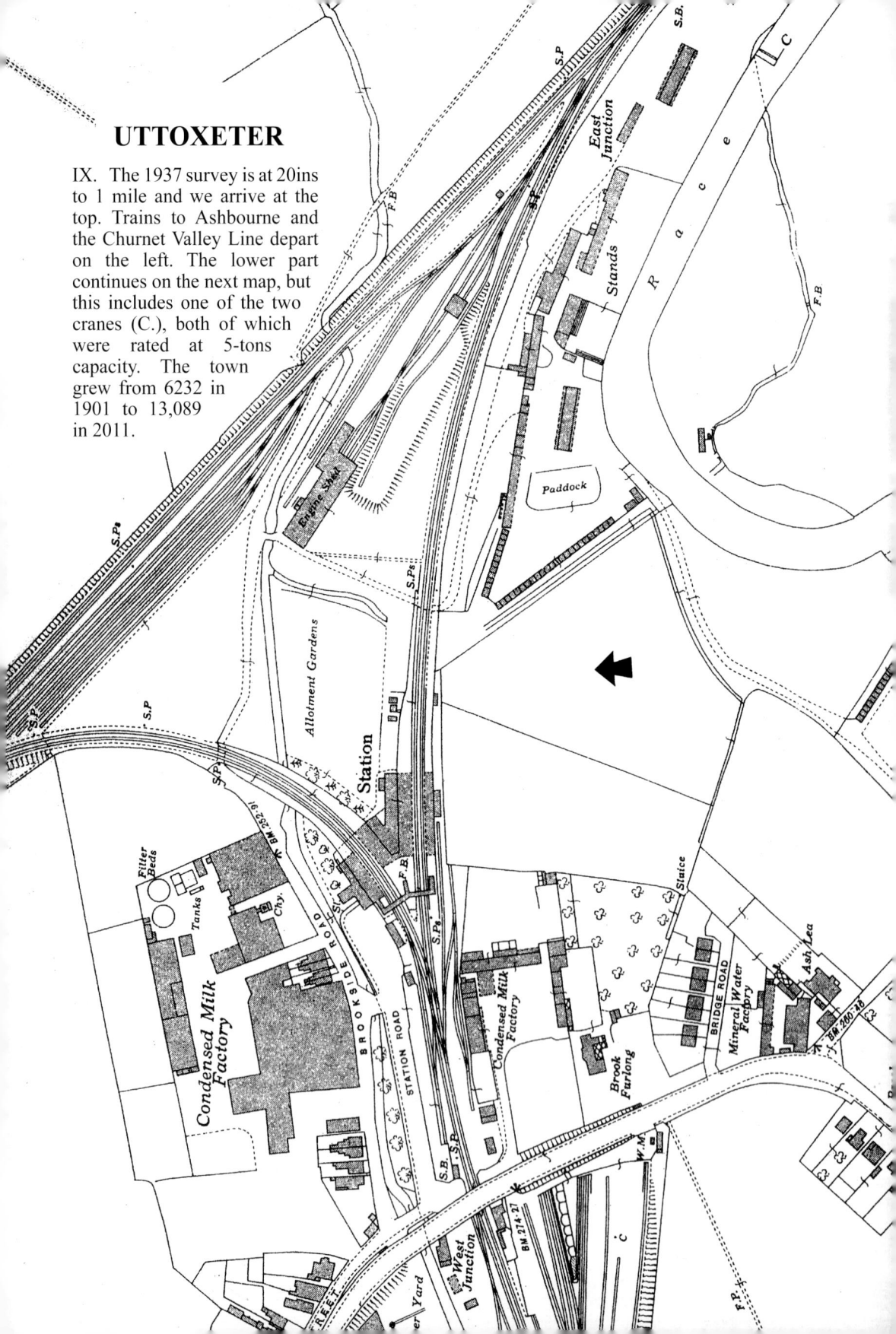

East Junction

Stands

Race

S.B.

C

F.B

F.B

S.P

S.P

S.Ps

S.P

S.P

Paddock

Engine Shed

S.Ps

Allotment Gardens

Station

S.Ps

Filter Beds

Tanks

Chy.

BM 252.91

F.B

Condensed Milk Factory

BROOKSIDE ROAD

STATION ROAD

Condensed Milk Factory

Brook Furlong

Sluice

Ash Lea

BRIDGE ROAD

Mineral Water Factory

BM 260.18

S.B.

S.P.

West Junction

BM 274.27

W.M.

C

F.P.

28.   We start with a fine panorama of all four platforms of the joint station, which was opened on 1st October 1881. Previously there had been a station at East Junction and another at Bridge Street, which is near the lower border of the map. A third was to the north, at Dove Bank. The latter and Junction station had opened on 13th July 1849. (LOSA)

29.   It is May 1948 and no. 2543 is waiting to depart north. It is a class 4P 2-6-4T, ex-LMS, from Stoke Shed. Modern electric lights have arrived. These tracks were lifted in 1968. Stephensons operated competitive bus services from 1926 to 1994, mostly under the title of "Yellow Buses". (W.A.Camwell/SLS)

30. The ex-NSR shed is seen on 24th April 1960. It was coded 5F from 1948, until closure in 1964. It had an allocation of six or seven locomotives in most of that period. (R.S.Carpenter)

31. We are looking towards East Junction, with the avoiding line in the background, in about September 1964. Passenger services on the Churnet Valley Line from Uttoxeter towards Leek and Macclesfield ceased operation on 2nd January 1965, and the trains towards Ashbourne and Buxton ended on 1st November 1954. (R.J.Essery/R.S.Carpenter coll.)

32. East Box is seen on the same visit. Opened in 1877, the frame had 26 levers and was in use until 16th March 1967. At ground level is the roofless coal store and the windowless toilet. The box controlled sidings for the BP & Shell Mex depot. After closure, a ground frame sufficed until May 1983, when oil traffic ended. (R.J.Essery/R.S.Carpenter)

33.   The prospective passenger's perspective is also from the same day. The station ceased to be staffed on 3rd May 1971 and the goods yard was closed on 2nd July 1973. All the buildings were later demolished to be replaced with simple platform shelters. (R.J.Essery/R.S.Carpenter coll.)

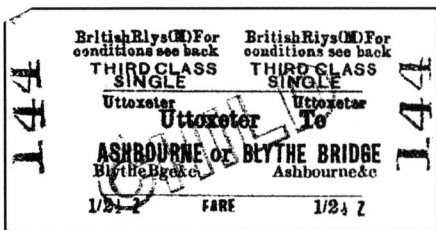

British Rlys(M) For conditions see back — THIRD CLASS SINGLE — Uttoxeter — Uttoxeter To — ASHBOURNE or BLYTHE BRIDGE — Blythe Bge&c — 1/2½ 2 — FARE

British Rlys(M) For conditions see back — THIRD CLASS SINGLE — Uttoxeter To — Uttoxeter — BLYTHE BRIDGE — Ashbourne&c — 1/2½ 2

T44   144

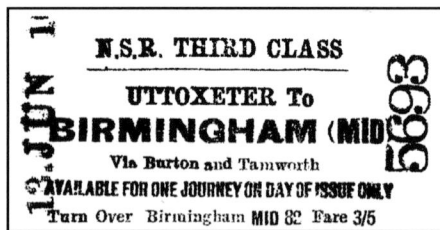

N.S.R. THIRD CLASS — UTTOXETER To — BIRMINGHAM (MID — Via Burton and Tamworth — AVAILABLE FOR ONE JOURNEY ON DAY OF ISSUE ONLY — Turn Over   Birmingham MID 82   Fare 3/5

19 JUN 1

5693

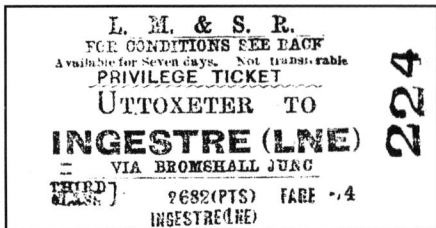

L. M. & S. R. — FOR CONDITIONS SEE BACK — Available for Seven days.   Not transferable — PRIVILEGE TICKET — UTTOXETER   TO — INGESTRE (LNE) — VIA BROMSHALL JUNC — THIRD   2682(PTS)   FARE  4 — INGESTRE(LNE)

224

This ticket is issued subject to the conditions on back hereof. N.S.R. Co. — PARLIAMENTARY — UTTOXETER To — LICHFIELD (CITY) — VIA BURTON — AVAILABLE ON DAY OF ISSUE FOR ONE JOURNEY ONLY — TURN OVER   Lichfield C 69   FARE 2s 1d

3520

34. No. 58038 passes through Uttoxeter station on 4th July 1986 with the 13.34 Toton-Garston Merry-go-round train, conveying coal for export through Garston Docks to Ireland. This was a major traffic flow in the 1980s, when the Irish power generators consumed fuel from the East Midlands and Yorkshire coalfields. Twenty years later the coal would be travelling through Uttoxeter in the opposite direction, with imports from Liverpool Docks to Ratcliffe power station. By 2016, no rail freight of any description was scheduled to pass through here. (P.D.Shannon)

35. The footbridge was completed in 2013 to avoid the use of the track crossing. Direct access to the racecourse was provided then. It is on the right. No. 153385 is working the 11.42 Derby to Crewe on 22nd April 2016. (A.C.Hartless)

**WEST OF UTTOXETER**

36. Two more photos from September 1964 enhance our survey. West Box was built in 1881 and named simply "Uttoxeter" from 16th March 1969 until closure on 18th November 1973. Lifting barriers arrived then, worked from Pinfold Crossing under CCTV. (R.J.Essery/R.S.Carpenter)

X.   The continuation of the previous map shows three signal boxes; top is West (40 levers, closed 18th November 1973), centre is Pinfold Crossing (31 levers, closed 9th January 1981) and lower is Hockley Crossing (20 levers, closed 25th January 1981). The short siding of the Anglo-American Oil Company is east of the middle one. The massive works has sidings entering both parts and a link between the two. They were owned by Bamford & Sons, makers of agricultural equipment. It was a descendant, with the initials J.C.B., who is well known for an even wider range of machines. Army staff cars were built here by Daimler during World War II and the sidings were then of great value. Bridge Street originally had a level crossing.

37. The ground frame was controlled by West Box signalman, using codes on the bell seen. The shunter had to respond, using the same system. Further west was Hockley Crossing Box. Lifting barriers had arrived in 1978.
(R.J.Essery/R.S.Carpenter)

38.  No. 47365 has been pressed into service to haul the 11.15 Manchester-Euston diverted via Uttoxeter, Castle Donington and St Pancras, in January 1984. A van stands at the disused dock. The box on the left had 40 levers and opened on 9th January 1981, replacing Hockley Crossing Box. It took on the work of the other nearby boxes and also barrier control here. The goods yard closed on 1st July 1982. (N.Allsop)

39.  It is 16th April 2012 and no. 66136 passes with coal from Liverpool Docks to Ratcliffe Power Station. The box was the last mechanical one built by the LMR. It was still in use in 2016. (P.D.Shannon)

# BROMSHALL

40. Passing Bromshall Junction in the early 1950s is ex-LMS class 5 4-6-0 no. 44819. It is probably working an express at holiday time. The 19-lever box was in use from 1878 to 5th June 1966. The rusty rails carried goods trains to Stafford until 1951. Another junction called just Bromshall was laid in 1942 to serve a ROD store for munitions. Its 20-lever box lasted until 21st May 1967 from when the junction was controlled from Hockley Crossing Box. The siding was closed in December 1968. There was a temporary station from May to September 1942 for construction workers. (W.A.Camwell/SLS)

41. The rusty lines in the previous picture became a single track after a short distance. Their junction had been controlled by the 1881 Bromshall West Junction Box until its closure in 1925. It is seen in terminal decline on 23rd March 1957. The train is the SLS tour, the last train over the route. It reversed here, as the junction had been taken out of use. We continue our journey to Stafford at picture 84. (R.M.Casserley)

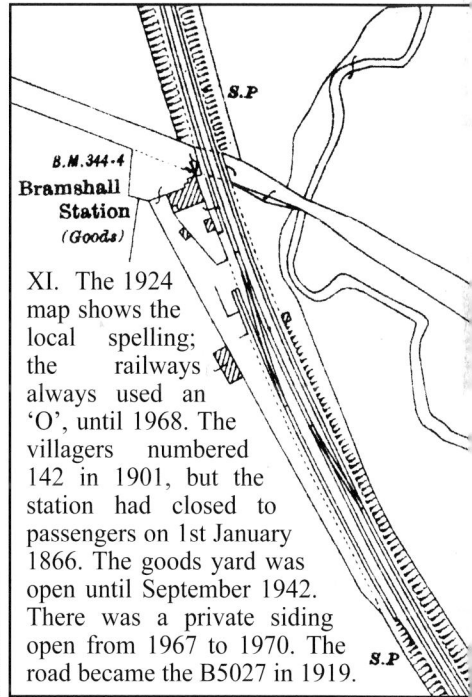

XI. The 1924 map shows the local spelling; the railways always used an 'O', until 1968. The villagers numbered 142 in 1901, but the station had closed to passengers on 1st January 1866. The goods yard was open until September 1942. There was a private siding open from 1967 to 1970. The road became the B5027 in 1919.

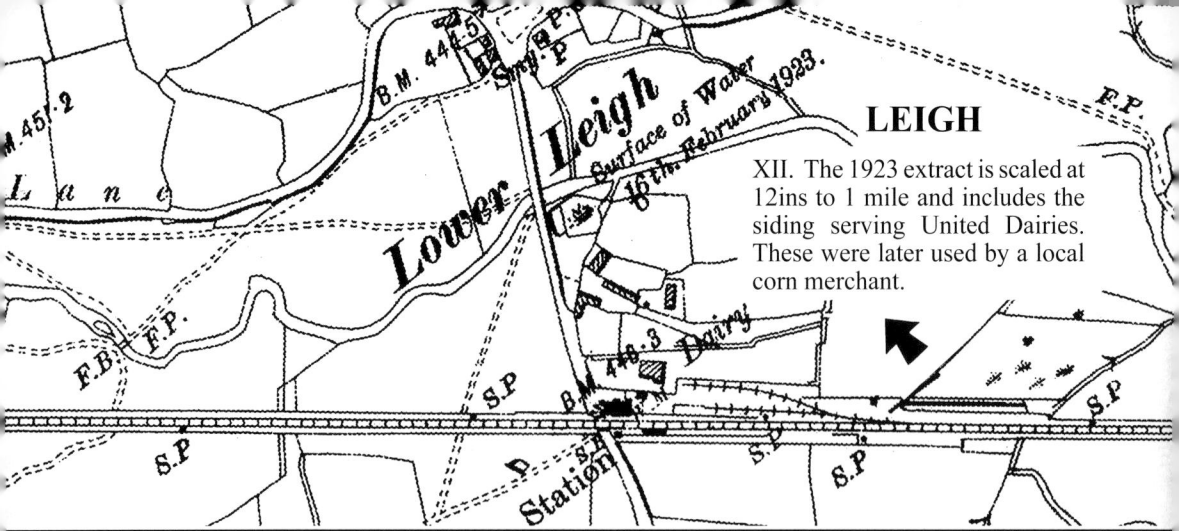

LEIGH

XII. The 1923 extract is scaled at 12ins to 1 mile and includes the siding serving United Dairies. These were later used by a local corn merchant.

42.   With a dairy so close to the station, churns were inevitable and very noisy when empty. Local residents numbered 853 in 1901. (LOSA)

43.   A postcard view towards Uttoxeter includes a multitude of cattle wagons, plus more evidence of rural paraffin lighting. The goods yard was in use until 7th December 1964; it had a 5-ton crane listed in 1938. (LOSA)

44. This view west is from late 1964 and it includes a refuge siding, not shown on the map. The 1892 signal box had 26 levers and closed on 12 July 1999. (R.J.Essery/R.S.Carpenter coll.)

45. One of the earliest batch of Sprinter units, no. 150107, passes Leigh box with the 13.09 Derby-Crewe service on 4th July 1986. Leigh station had closed to passengers on 7th November 1966. This became the last surviving mechanically driven gated level crossing on former NSR lines. After closure, the box was moved to a nearby industrial yard, where it was used as an office for several years. (P.D.Shannon)

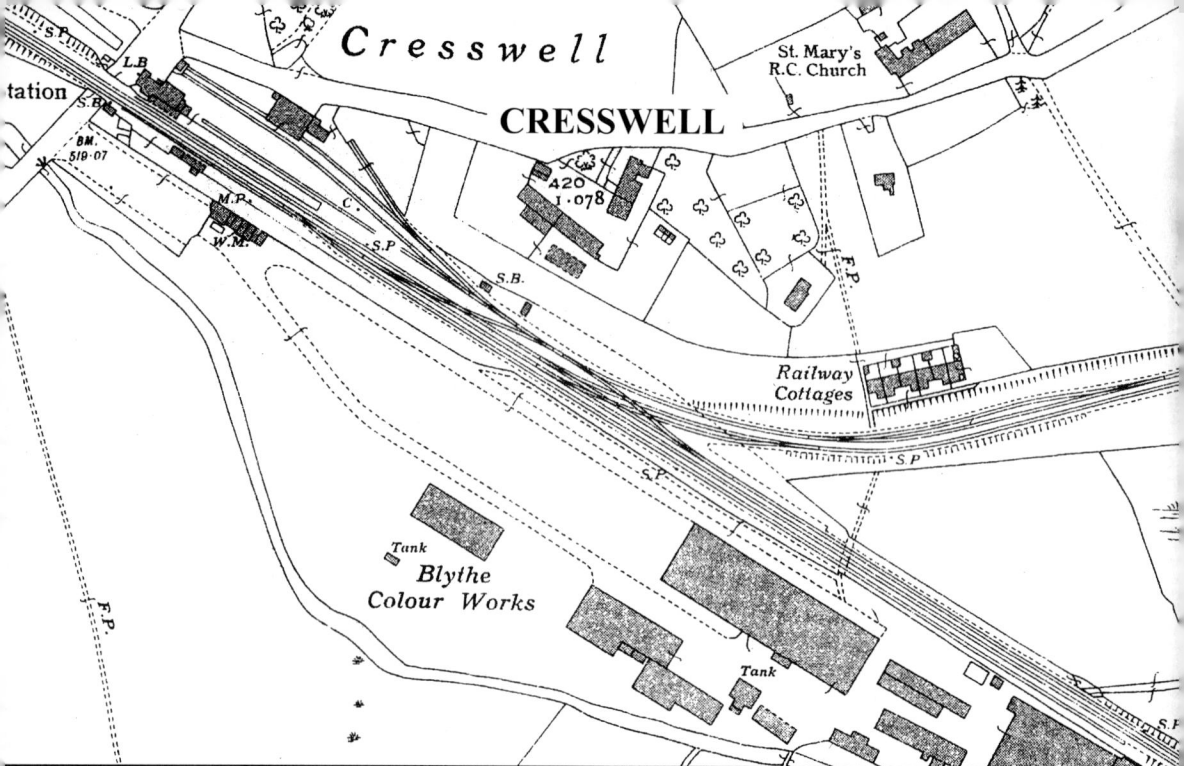

Cresswell

CRESSWELL

St. Mary's
R.C. Church

Railway
Cottages

Blythe
Colour Works

Tank

XIII.   The 1937 edition at 20ins to 1 mile has a long siding close to the works, with a footpath passing over all the tracks and through its yard. The crane (C.) was of 2½ ton capacity. The Cheadle Branch curves to the right.

46.     Yard Box contained a ground frame and is left of the centre of the map. Many levers can be seen inside and two weighted (automatic) levers can be seen outside. The box lasted until 1930. (P.Laming coll.)

47.     The village had only 46 residents in 1901, but an impressive facade. This was the only station on the route with the luxury of pantiles and is seen in 1952. (Bentley coll.)

48.     Two photographs from 28th May 1961 enhance our survey. This one reveals another elaborate barge board, plus fine finials. Passenger service was withdrawn here on 7th November 1966. (Milepost 92½)

49.     The factory siding on the right doubled as a refuge siding. The one on the left is doing likewise, with coal hoppers taking a rest. Local goods traffic ceased on 4th January 1965, but sand from the Cheadle branch, via the sidings, continued until 1984. (Milepost 92½)

50.   The platform running-in boards carried the words "Change for Tean and Cheadle" until 1963. The box had 31 levers and was in use from 1892 to 18th March 1989, when automatic half barriers came into use. The photo is from 1964. (R.J.Essery/R.S.Carpenter coll.)

# WEST OF CRESSWELL

51. No. 150129 is working the 10.38 Crewe to Derby on 11th August 1988. The lane runs south for a mile before reaching the gates of Stallington Hall. The 1884 box had 14 levers and lasted until 18th March 1989, when half barriers arrived, controlled from Caverswall. (A.C.Hartless)

# BLYTHE BRIDGE

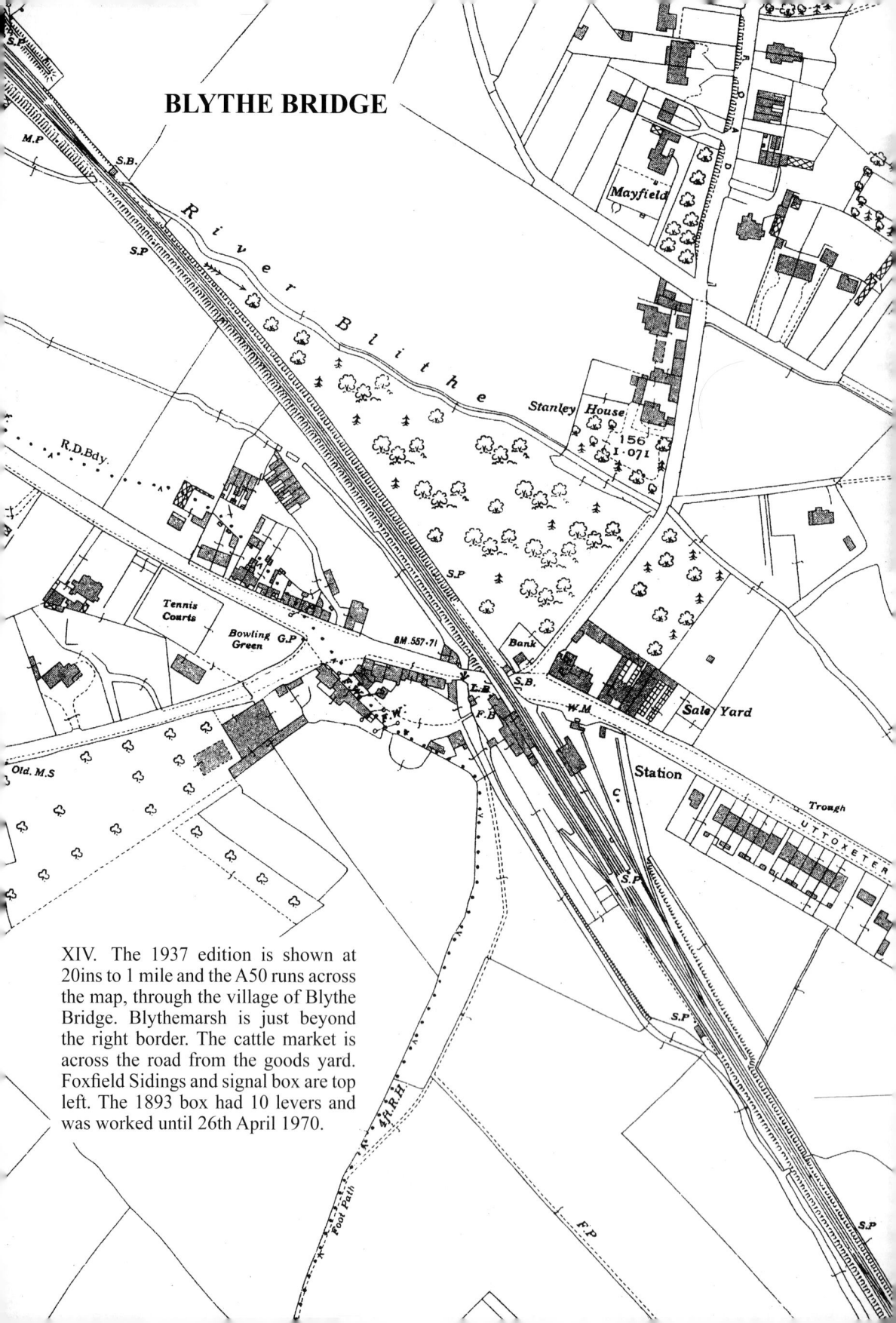

Mayfield

*River Blithe*

S.P

M.P

S.B.

S.P

R.D.Bdy.

Stanley House

156
1·071

S.P

Tennis
Courts

Bowling
Green

G.P

Bank

S.B.

Old. M.S

BM.557·71

L.B.

F.B.

F.W.

W.M.

Sale Yard

Station

C.

S.P

Trough

UTTOXETER

S.P

S.P

S.P

Foot Path

F.P

XIV. The 1937 edition is shown at
20ins to 1 mile and the A50 runs across
the map, through the village of Blythe
Bridge. Blythemarsh is just beyond
the right border. The cattle market is
across the road from the goods yard.
Foxfield Sidings and signal box are top
left. The 1893 box had 10 levers and
was worked until 26th April 1970.

52.     Some staff are nonchalant as NSR no. 48 arrives from Stoke. The engine is an NSR class L 0-6-2T. It became LMS class 3F no. 2273. The signal box had a gate wheel. (P.Laming coll.)

53.     The ornate south elevation with its patterned brickwork and bold crest plate was photographed on 6th September 1965. The level crossing is on the left. Its gates were replaced by full barriers in 1966. They were under CCTV from Caverswall Box, to the west, from March 1980. These buildings vanished in the 1990s. (R.J.Essery/R.S.Carpenter coll.)

54.    The up platform is seen on the same day, with the gates in full. Unusually, the waiting room is in an extension of the goods shed. Freight traffic ceased here on 4th January 1965. The 20-lever box of 1884 functioned until 16th March 1980. (R.J.Essery/R.S.Carpenter coll.)

55.    It is 11th August 1988. Second generation DMUs have now taken over, and for a while there were some more adventurous through travel opportunities. This is no. 150110 arriving with the 07.08 Holyhead to Derby. The relic on the left is seen in full in picture 52. There is now no trace. (A.C.Hartless)

56.     Single car no. 153376 calls at Blythe Bridge working the 16.42 Derby-Crewe service on 24th March 2016. The goods shed remains in commercial use in 2016. The Best Small Station award was received here from East Midlands Trains in 2010. Passenger numbers rose from 60,162 that year to 78,470 in 2014. (P.D.Shannon)

# WEST OF BLYTHE BRIDGE

57.     Pictured on 24th March 2016, Caverswall box was opened by the LMS in 1942 to control two goods loops that had been installed for increased wartime traffic. It had 35 levers. The level crossing gates were replaced by lifting barriers in 1983, but the box survived into the 21st century, having taken over the remote control of crossings at Blythe Bridge, Stallington, Cresswell, Upper Leigh and Leigh. Caverswall never had a station, the nearest being Meir just under ½ mile further west. (P.D.Shannon)

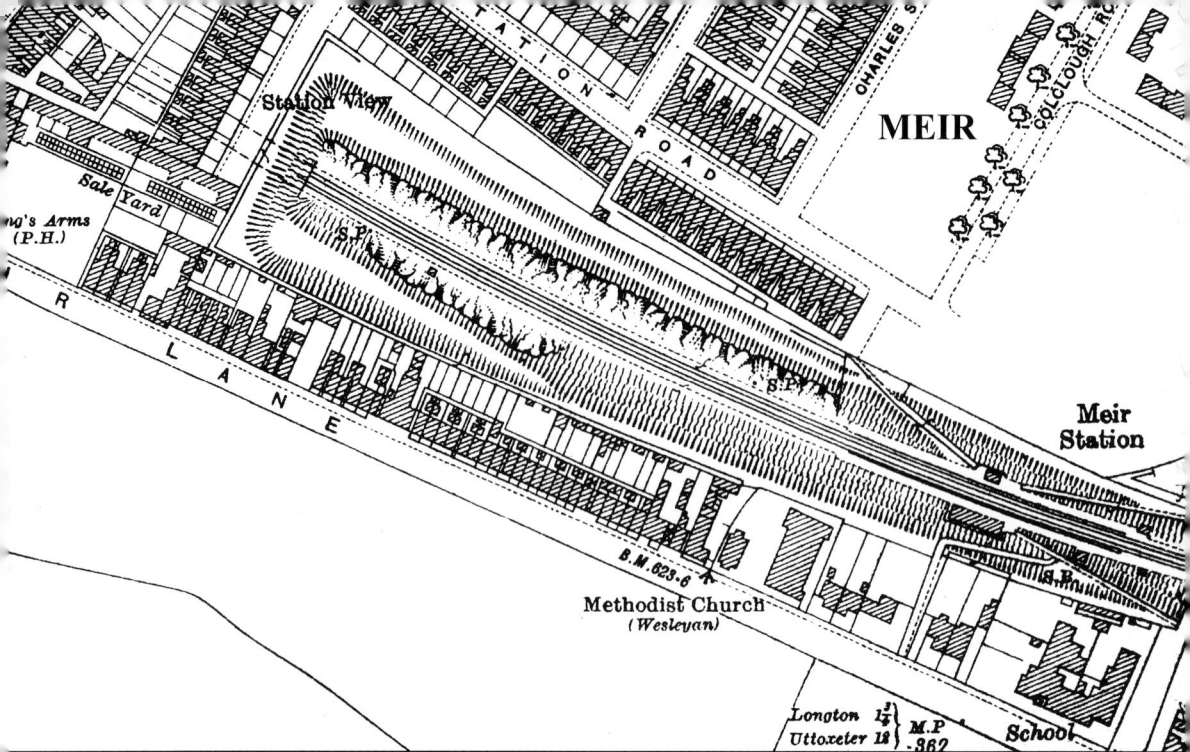

The 1927 map of Meir Station area showing Station Road, Meir Station, Methodist Church (Wesleyan), Sale Yard, King's Arms (P.H.), and milepost markings: Longton 1¾, Uttoxeter 18, M.P. 362.

XV.  The 1927 issue reveals that the station was by then in the suburbs of Stoke and it had access by four footpaths. It opened on 12th May 1894, much later than most on the route. Unclear is the 12-lever signal box, which was in use from 1894 to 1936.

58.  A local train is about to enter the 814 yard long Meir Tunnel on 4th November 1957. A popular website states that the toilet bucket at Meir was emptied by the junior porter into a hole he dug between the shrubs behind the station. The station closed on 7th November 1966. The bridge carried the A520. (Milepost 92½)

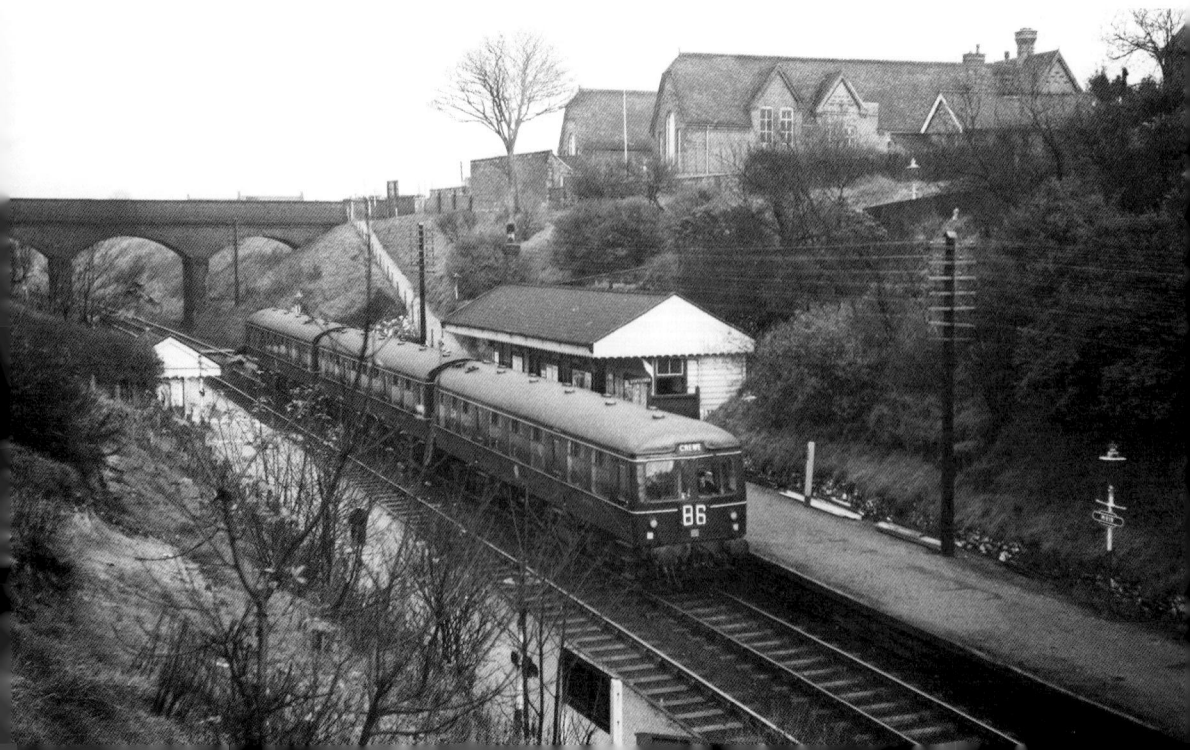

# NORMACOT

59.   Seen in NSR days, the station had steps and ramps down to the platforms. It closed to passengers on 2nd March 1964; it had no goods facilities. The 22-lever signal box of 1882 was named Normacot Junction from 1892 until closure on 15th August 1965. The next west was at Millfield Crossing (12 levers, 1916-1962) and then came Bridgewoods Sidings (25 levers, 1928-1970). (P.Laming coll.)

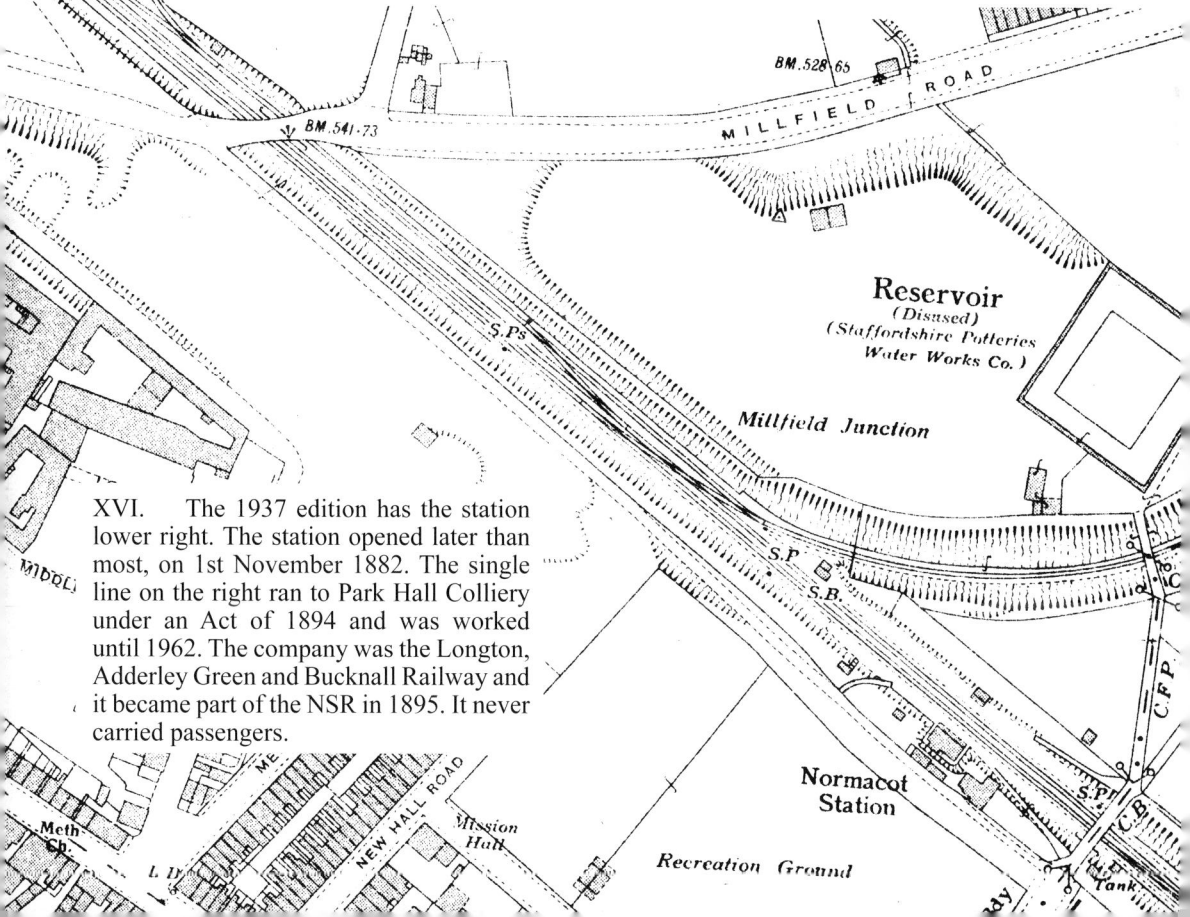

XVI.    The 1937 edition has the station lower right. The station opened later than most, on 1st November 1882. The single line on the right ran to Park Hall Colliery under an Act of 1894 and was worked until 1962. The company was the Longton, Adderley Green and Bucknall Railway and it became part of the NSR in 1895. It never carried passengers.

**LONGTON**

Foley
Place

Foley Potteries
(China & Earthenware)

B.M. 471·1

B.M. 461·8

Goods Shed

S.P.

S.P.

B.M. 474·0

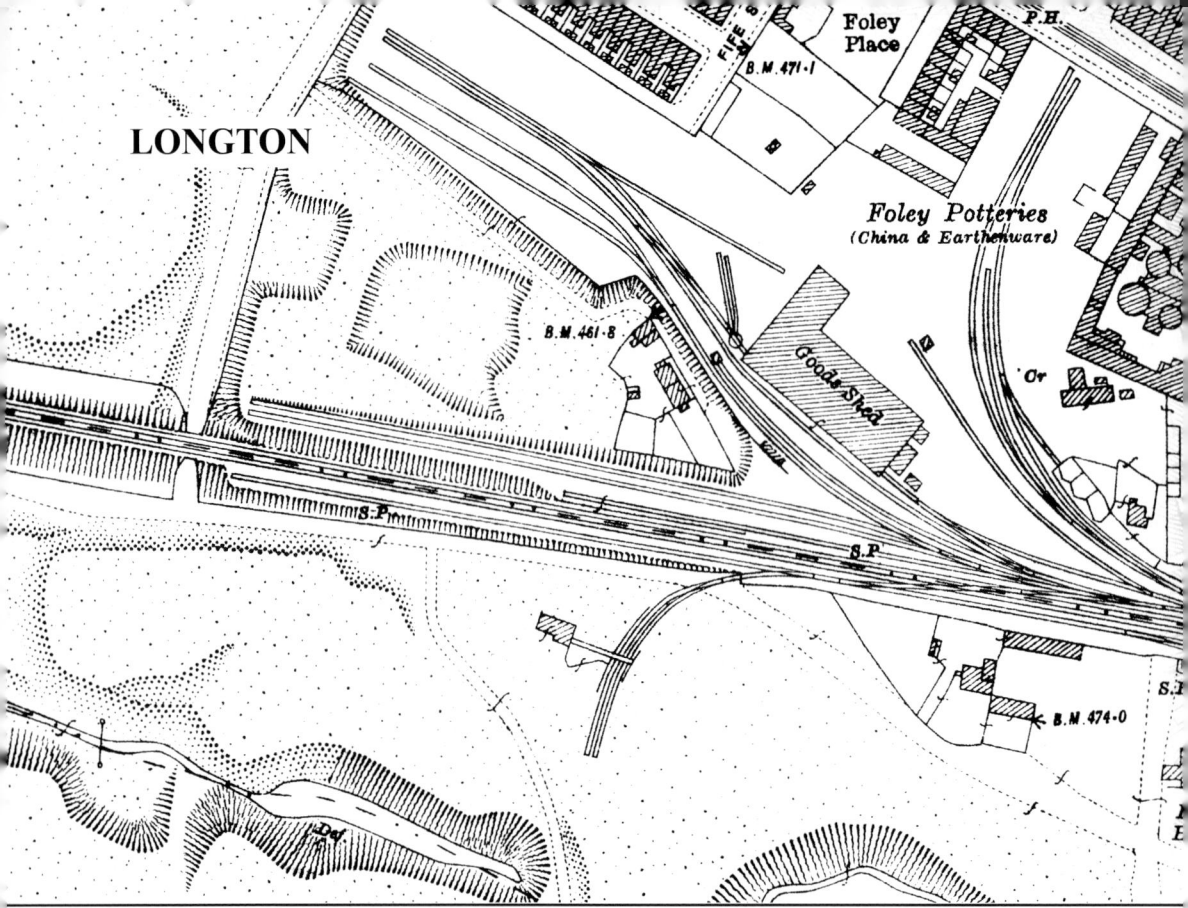

60. The roof over the platforms on the left was renewed in 1938. Note the curved tram track connection, incomplete on the map, and the offset signal post. The station became partially unstaffed in 1971. (LOSA)

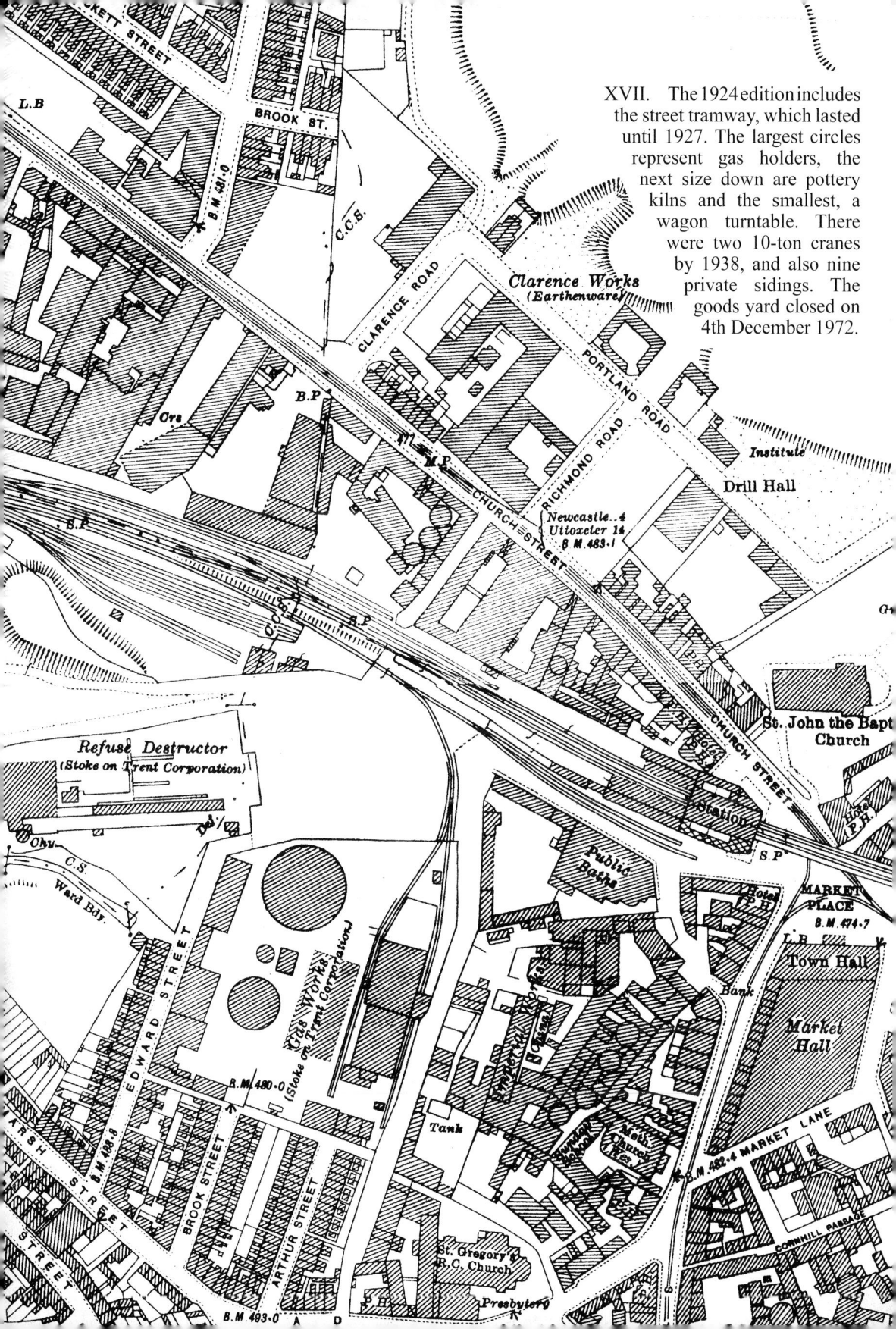

XVII. The 1924 edition includes the street tramway, which lasted until 1927. The largest circles represent gas holders, the next size down are pottery kilns and the smallest, a wagon turntable. There were two 10-ton cranes by 1938, and also nine private sidings. The goods yard closed on 4th December 1972.

BROOK ST.

L.B

B.M 481.0

C.C.S.

CLARENCE ROAD

Clarence Works
(Earthenware)

PORTLAND ROAD

B.P

Ore

RICHMOND ROAD

Institute

Drill Hall

M.P

CHURCH STREET

Newcastle..4
Uttoxeter 14
B.M 483.1

B.P

B.P

St. John the Bapt
Church

Refuse Destructor
(Stoke on Trent Corporation)

Station

S.P

Chy.

C.S.

Ward Bdy.

Public
Baths

Hotel
P.H.

MARKET
PLACE
B.M 474.7

L.B

Town Hall

EDWARD STREET

Gas Works
(Stoke on Trent Corporation)

Bank

Market
Hall

B.M 480.0

BROOK STREET

ARTHUR STREET

Tank

B.M 483.8

B.M 482.4 MARKET LANE

MARSH STREET

STREET

St. Gregory's
R.C. Church

CORNHILL PASSAGE

B.M 483.0

P.H.

Presbytery

A    D

61.  No. 153383's next stop is Stoke and it is loading on 1st May 2013. Both platforms had been resurfaced to serve four coaches. Bottle kilns remain to impress the town's history on visitors. There was a signal box on the platform from 1870 to 1936. Passenger numbers were around 60,000 per annum in 2012-14. (J.Whitehouse)

62.  Some attempt has been made to cheer up the unstaffed station, with daffodils sprouting among the shrubs on the eastbound platform and railway-inspired paintings on the boundary wall. Single car no. 153374 makes its call with the 15.42 Derby-Crewe service on 24th March 2016. Longton is well-situated for the town that it serves and in 2003 a new bus station was built next to it, grandly named the Longton Transport Interchange. Foley Crossing (pedestrians only) is 15 chains west of Longton. The cabin was built in 1889 and its 37-lever frame was still in use in 2016. (P.D.Shannon)

# FENTON

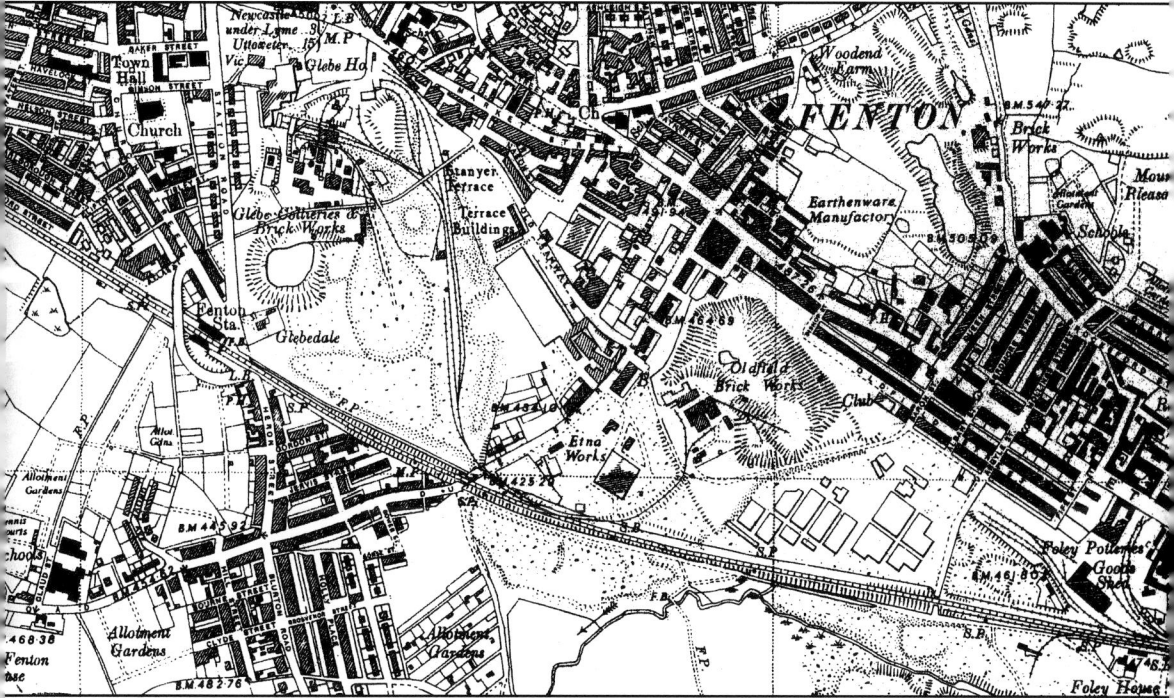

XVIII.   This revision from 1947 is at 6ins to 1 mile and has Glebe Colliery just north of the station. The mine was sunk in 1850 and was worked until November 1964.

63.   Passenger service began on 1st August 1864, but a new station was opened on 31st October 1906, west of the main road. The original one is seen, together with its level crossing, which was replaced by a bridge in 1906. (A.Dudman coll.)

64. The later station and its new footbridge is pictured. Regular passenger service was withdrawn on 1st June 1961, but some Wakes Week trains called in 1962. (A.Dudman coll.)

65. The output of Glebe Colliery was enormous; 1947 being an example with 172,217 tons. It had its own shunting locomotives and they marshalled two complete trains daily for many years. The 20-lever box was named Fenton Sidings from 1899 until closure in 1966. (A.Dudman coll.)

# SOUTH OF STOKE-ON-TRENT

66.  This small shed was added in 1905, when steam railmotors came into use on local services. The main sheds can be found in pictures 106-109 in *Rugeley to Stoke-on-Trent*. LMS class G2a 0-8-0 no. 9237 is seen on 22nd May 1932. (H.C.Casserley)

# STOKE-ON-TRENT

67.  The use of three words in the name started in 1910, when the County Borough was created. A temporary station was in use until this fine structure opened on 9th October 1848. The King brought city status here in 1926. (A.Dudman coll.)

XIX. Stoke Junction is on the right and we arrive on the lower line, the upper one running to Leek. At the lower border is the track carrying Stafford trains. Its signal box had 128 levers and lasted until 17th July 1966, when the new power signal box took over the district. This is the 1947 revision at 6ins to 1 mile, with the circular and rectangular engine sheds on opposite sides of Stoke Junction. Top left are Cockshute Sidings, which were used for DMUs from 1957 to 1966, when electrification took place. Steam ceased and the shed closed on 7th August 1967, the round house being demolished in 1970. Locomotive building took place here from 1868 to 1926.

68.	Not evident in the previous view is the protruding first floor section, which accommodated the board room and gave the NSR directors good lighting. This Jacobean joy could be seen from the front rooms of the North Stafford Hotel. This ceased to be railway property in 1953. (P.Laming coll.)

69.	Original gas lighting is included in this early postcard view of the smoke ducting. The quarter circle structures are pipes for locomotive water. The two centre roads were used mainly for empty coaches between trips. (P.Laming coll.)

Station. Stoke.

70. No. 304037 is working from Manchester to Stafford on 31st August 1981 and is entering the 13-coach up platform. The down one takes 14 and the bay (left) suits four. The down through line had been lifted to make way for electrification masts. (T.Heavyside)

**STOKE** (Junction).

A telegraph station.

HOTELS.—Railway, Talbot.

BANKERS.—Moore and Co. (Weekly).

This is the busy capital of the *Staffordshire Potteries*, a district 9 miles long, including *Longton, Fenton, Hanley, Burslem, Etruria, Tunstall,* &c., which, with other places, are incorporated within the new borough, containing a population of 101,207, who return two members, nearly all employed in the manufacture of pottery, or the arts connected with it. Potters' clay (though of a coarse quality) and coal are both abundant; hence the peculiar advantages hitherto possessed by this spot. Stout low kilns, like the martello towers in Kent, are smoking about everywhere; each the centre of a pottery establishment, for which a "Bank" is the local name. Copeland's Bank, for instance, means Copeland's Works. At these, and at Minton's, are produced the most beautiful porcelain, rivalling the best made abroad; also the terra cotta, tesselated tiles, &c., so extensively used in new churches, and the small figures, in imitation of marble statuary.

At Stoke, the principal buildings are, a modern *Town Hall,* vast *Railway Station,* built in the Tudor style, at a cost of £150,000. The approaches are paved with Minton's tiles; new *Church,* in which are the tombs of Wedgwood and Spode, two eminent names in this locality. Wedgwood died in 1795, at Etruria, so called because of his successful imitation of the ancient vases under that name, now the seat of one of his family. At *Stoke,* or *Fenton Manor House,* Fenton, the poet, was born.

Bradshaw's Guide of 1866

**For other views of this station, see** *Branch Lines Around Market Drayton* **and** *Rugeley to Stoke-on-Trent via Stone.* **A 2010 cab ride DVD is available, called** *Derby to Crewe.*

71.  No. 50714 heads the class 120s working the 18.20 Crewe to Lincoln service on 3rd April 1983. The 1966 Stoke Power Signal Box is close to the class 47 diesel in the siding. On the left is North Yard Box, which controlled shunting until 9th December 1984. The 120-lever North Box of 1931 had closed in 1966. The siding in the foreground was known as the "Fish Dock". (A.C.Hartless)

72.  Nearest is no. 153383, which is working from Derby to Crewe on 5th June 2010. The second through line had become redundant by that time. The route becomes quadruple track north of the station, at Newcastle Junction. The roof of the subway is evident here. (J.Whitehouse)

# 2. Burton-on-Trent Branch

XX. The 1946 edition is at 2ins to 1 mile and has the junction for passengers at Tutbury, top left. The main line from Derby is on the right. The Dove flows into the Trent east of Stretton.

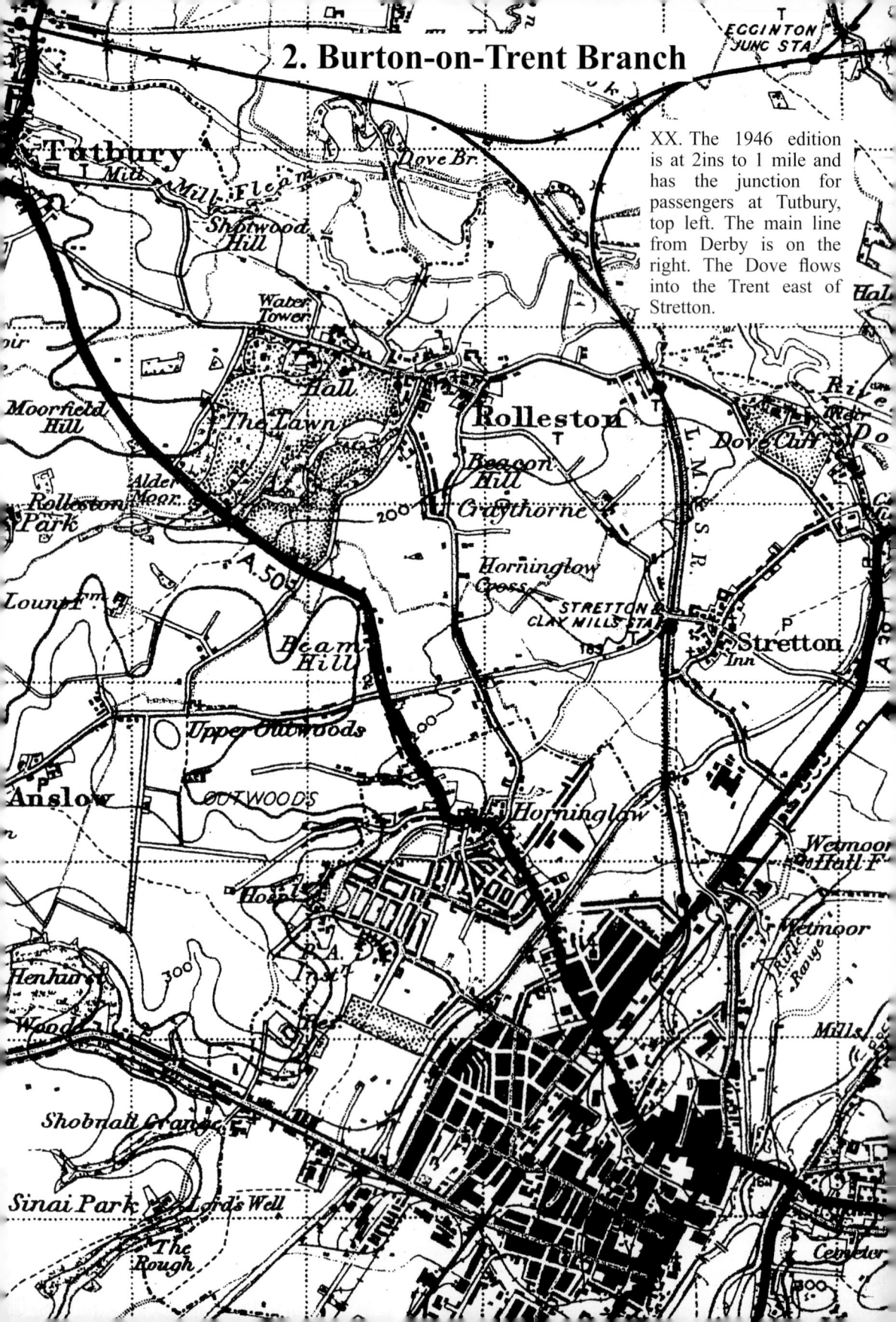

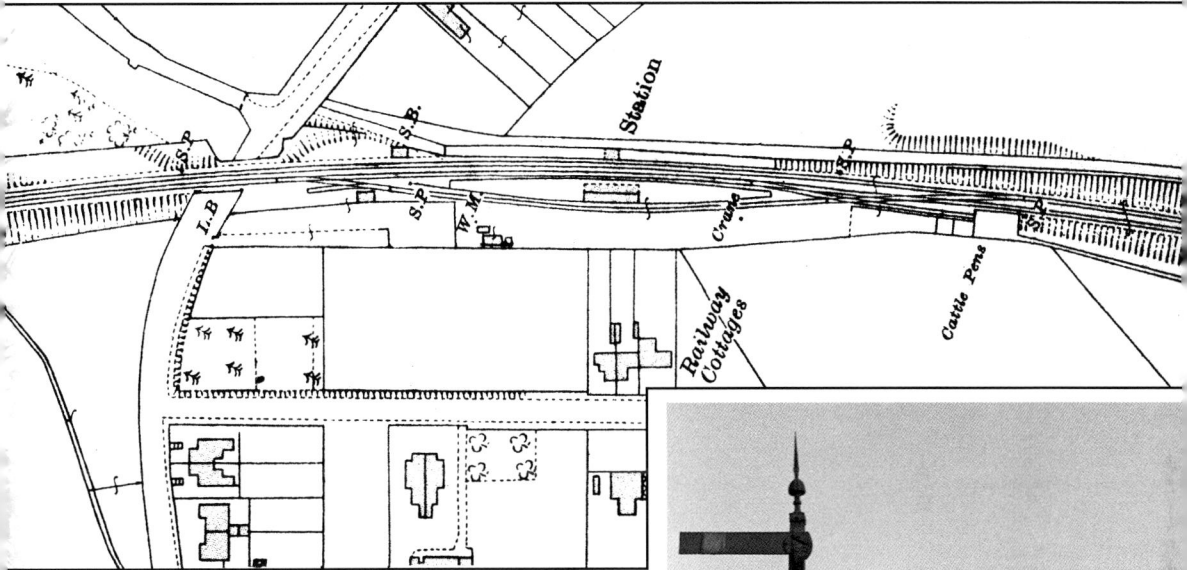

XXI.    The 1923 survey features the first station south of the River Dove on the Burton link line of 1848. The crane shown was rated at 5 tons.

73.  We are looking south on 31st July 1954 at the station, which did not open until 1st November 1894. The signal box had 26 levers and opened at about the same time as the station. It closed on 21st October 1951, as did the goods yard. Note that the lamp glasses are remote from the signal arm. The route was in use until 1968, for freight northwards. (J.P.Wilson/RAS)

74.  The goods loop ran behind the building on the right and ended near the cattle dock, in the distance. The British Tyre & Rubber Co. had private sidings here. The Jinnie Trail was created for walkers on the trackbed, although the train was usually known as the Ginny. (A.Dudman coll.)

# STRETTON & CLAYMILLS

XXII. The station location is revealed on map XX. This is the 1923 extract. The signal box shown was in use from 1922 to 1st May 1955. It had 15 levers. A goods loop was added to the north of the platforms in 1920 and it was used until 7th June 1965.

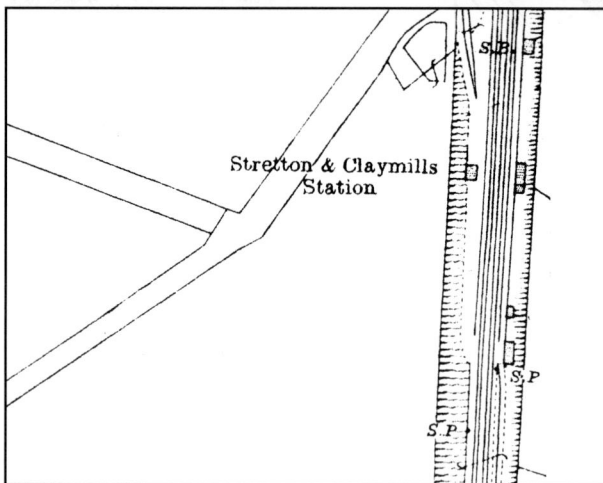

75. The platforms were brought into use on 1st August 1901 and this postcard would have been produced soon after, but within the long skirt era. The route was used by freight trains between London (Camden) and Carlisle for some years. (LOSA)

76. The 5.35pm Tutbury to Burton train is being propelled south on 5th August 1959 by no. 41277, a class 2MT 2-6-2T. The buildings were demolished in 1964. Clay Mills village is on the right border of map XX. (R.J.Buckley/Initial Photographics)

Horninglow Station

ETON ROAD

DERBY ROAD

S.B.

S.B.

Chy.

Malthouse

A.38

L.B.

S.P.

BM.151·89

BM 153.64

Allotment Gardens

S.P.

BM.150.68

S.P.

S.P.

**HORNINGLOW**

B.M.149·7
F.B.

S.Ps

Burt
North Ju

S.B.

M.P.

Ward Bay.

C.R.

S.P.

S.P.

S.Ps

Meth. Chapel
(Primitive)

N.S.R.
HORNINGLOW BRANCH

C.R.

Ward Bay

L

P.H

S.P.

Wetmore Sidings

S.P.

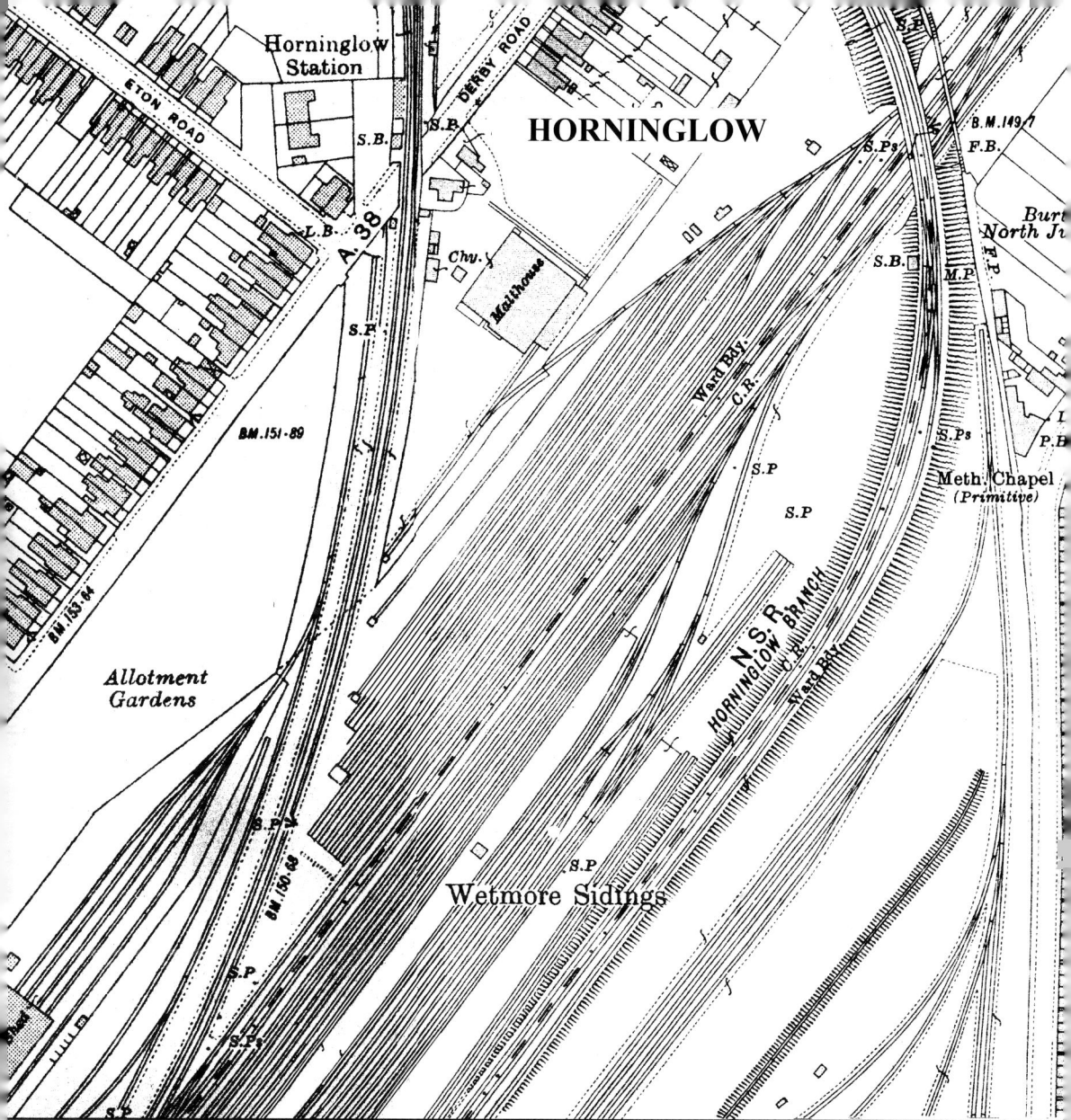

XXIII. The 1922 extract has the station at the top left. The back cover diagram helps to explain the destinations of the lines.

77. The platforms are seen from the A38 in 1951. After line closure, the building was converted into a café. The up platform shelter arrived in 1888. On the right is the wicket gate for pedestrians.
(R.M.Casserley coll.)

78. The tiny box had 9 levers, which were in use from 1895 until 3rd April 1966, when the line to Tutbury closed. Some spotters watched a diesel shunter pass with a few wagons, on that sad day. This photo is from 1957. (R.S.Carpenter)

79. The former GNR and NSR engine shed is beyond the massive water tank, which spans two roads. One is higher than the other to facilitate coaling of locomotives. Class 4F 0-6-0 no. 44248 is leaving with freight for Mold Junction, in North Wales. (P.Webb coll.)

# BURTON-ON-TRENT

Black Eagle Brewery

Baptist Tabernacle

New Brewery

Malthouses

Malthouse

Middle Brewery

Salvation Army Barracks

Saw Mill

New Brewery

Station Hotel

Bank

Corn Mill

Pumping Station

Station

Tannery

Cooperage

Pumping Station

Malthouses

L. & N. W. R. Goods Depot

Kottingham Cooperage

Chapel

BROAD STREET

XXIV. The 1901 survey at 15ins to 1 mile features the centre of the brewery area, which developed steadily after the opening of the Trent & Mersey Canal in 1712. By 1869, there were 26 breweries with 16 miles of privately owned track, in addition to the railway owned tracks shown on the back cover.

80. This is the second station at Burton and it opened on 29th April 1883, having been built by the MR. The GNR had its own booking office therein. Tracks of the Burton Corporation Tramway (1903-29) are evident. The *Burton & Ashby Tramway* is the title of a Middleton Press album, which features other trams to appear here in 1906-27. Technically a Light Railway, it was opened and run by the MR. (P.Laming coll.)

81. This is Shobnall Junction, which is in the southwest area of the brewery lines. ex-MR 0-4-0T no. 1535 is hard at work on 27th June 1933, running towards Wellington Street Junction, which connects with the main lines. Alternatively, it may be going to Bond End Wharf. (H.C.Casserley)

82.   We are facing Bond End Wharf, which is at the southeast end of the system. With a main line train on 2nd June 1950 is class 4F 0-6-0 no. 44580 running south. Passing under it is class 0F 0-4-0ST no. 41523, which was ex-MR. (H.C.Casserley)

83.   Standing at Wellington Street coal stage on 2nd June 1957 is Bass no. 14. The curve on the right takes trains into the sidings. The line on the left is in the foreground of picture no. 81. Wellington Street Junction Box is in the background. (P.Webb/R.J.Essery coll.)

> **For other views and diagrams, see**
> *Tamworth to Derby* **(pictures 33 to 65)** and
> *Leicester to Burton* **(pictures 93 to 105).**

# 3. Grindley to Stafford

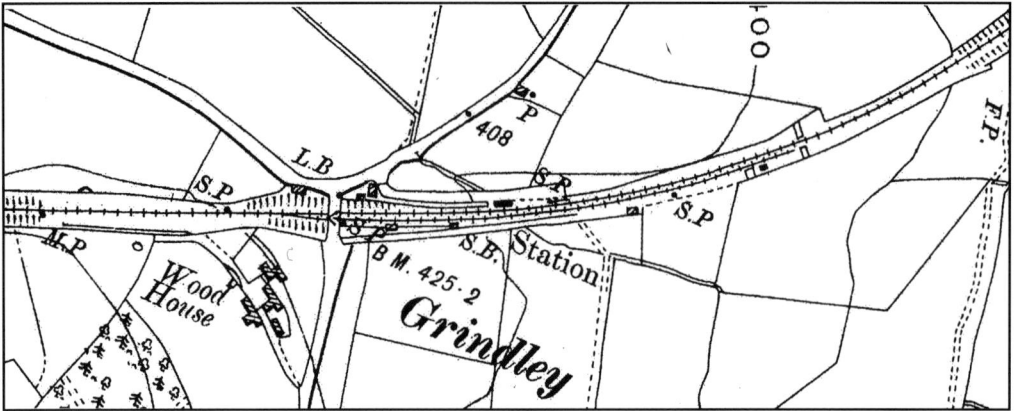

XXV. The 1922 survey is shown at 12ins to 1 mile. A passing loop and second platform had been added in 1887. The goods yard closed on 5th May 1951.

XXVI. The 1946 edition is at 1ins to 1 mile and has the main line from Rugeley to Stone on the right of the left page. Passing over it (top right) is the ex-GNR single line from Uttoxeter to Stafford, the former being top right on the right page. Ingestre station is shown close to the Trent & Mersey Canal, just on the left page. Passenger service had ceased on the route on 4th December 1939.

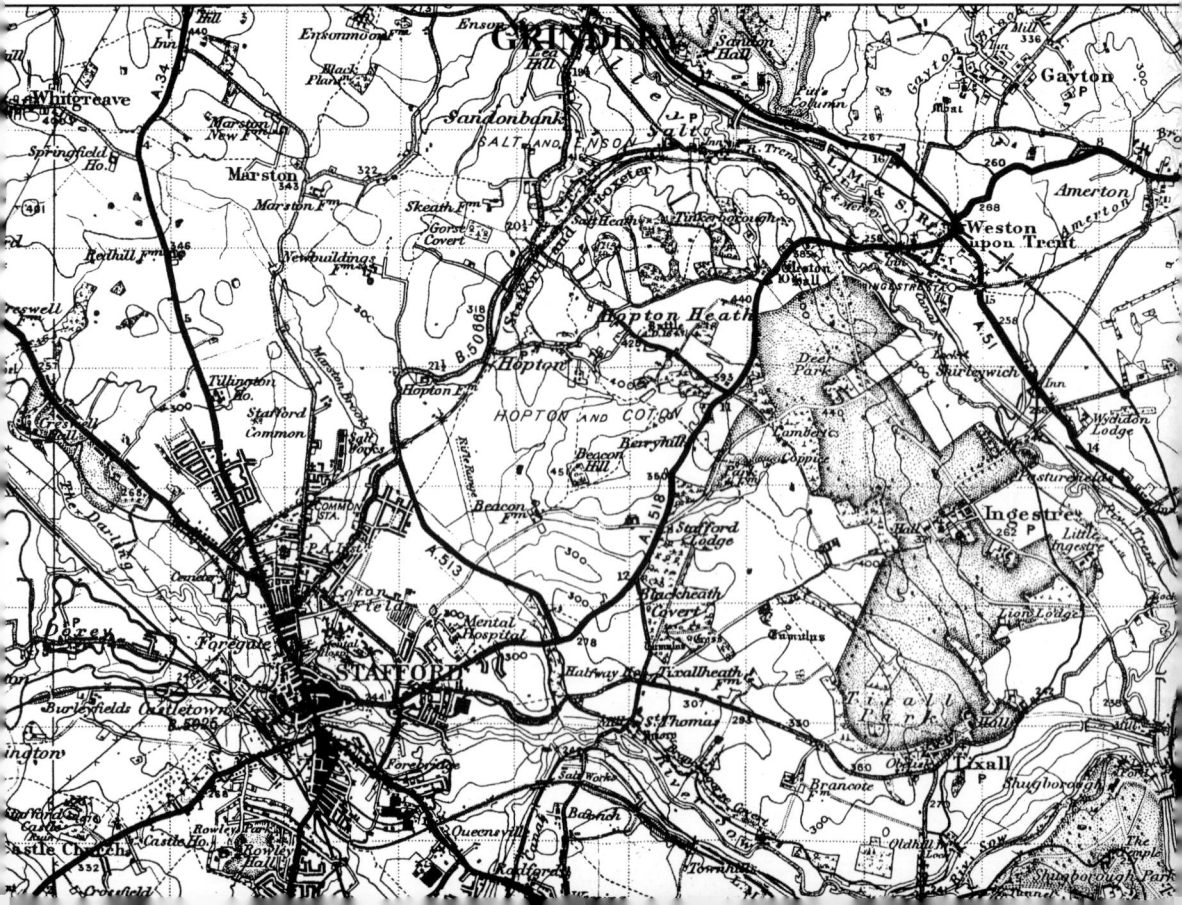

84. We look north in about the late 1950s; the track was lifted in 1959. There had been a 16-lever signal box here until 5th May 1951. (A.Dudman coll.)

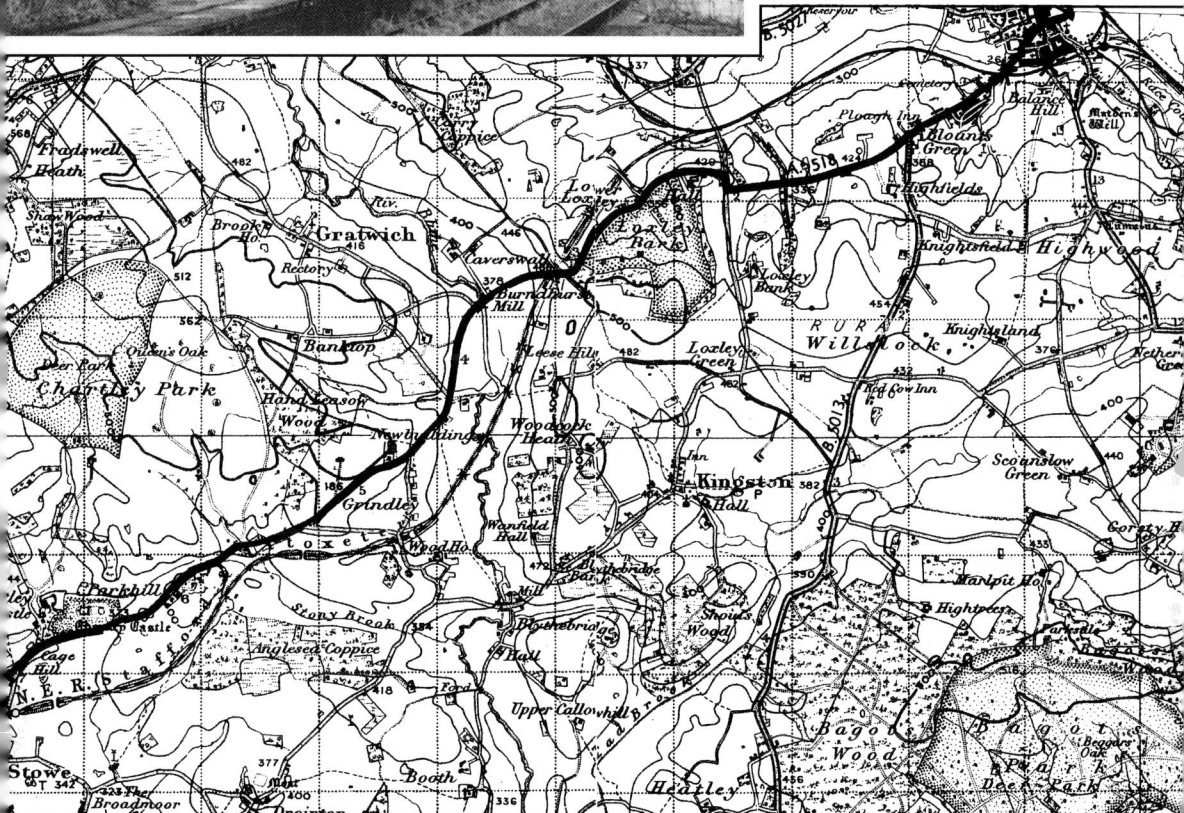

85. The edge of the loop platform was put to good use on 23rd March 1957, when the final train movement took place. Track lifting soon started. The SLS organised the memorable trip, which was from Stafford to Bromshall Junction and back. (R.M.Casserley)

# CHARTLEY

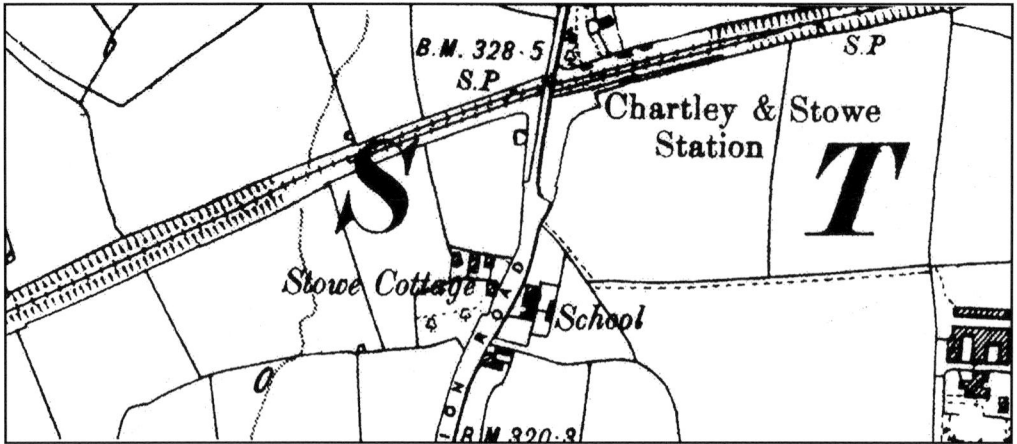

XXVII. Scaled at 12ins to 1 mile, this extract is from 1921. The 19-lever signal box is not marked, although in use from 1882 to 1951, although just a ground frame from 1942. The station was named STOWE until 3rd October 1874, but appears here with both words.

86. The same train is seen again as we look towards Bromshall Tunnel. There was always a spelling difference. Its length was 321 yards. (R.M.Casserley)

# INGESTRE

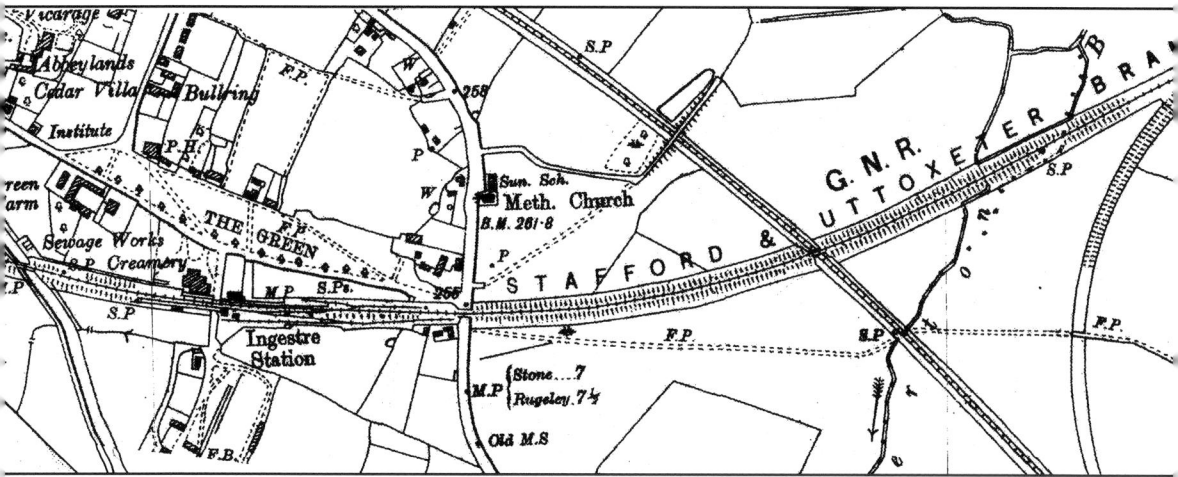

XXVIII.   The 1922 edition is at 6ins to 1 mile and reveals the route of a proposed connection to the main line. The station was called WESTON until January 1870.

87.   A southward view features the creamery on the right and the gateway to the station approach. The station building is partly behind the dwellings. (P.Laming coll.)

88.   The signal box was at the end of the platform for westbound trains. It had 25 levers and is seen neglected after line closure. The village had its population drop from 120 in 1901 to 116 in 1961. (A.Dudman coll.)

89.   We witness the 1957 SLS tour again, complete with the suffix, which was seldom used on paper. The raised section of platform was probably created for milk churns. (R.M.Casserley)

# SALT

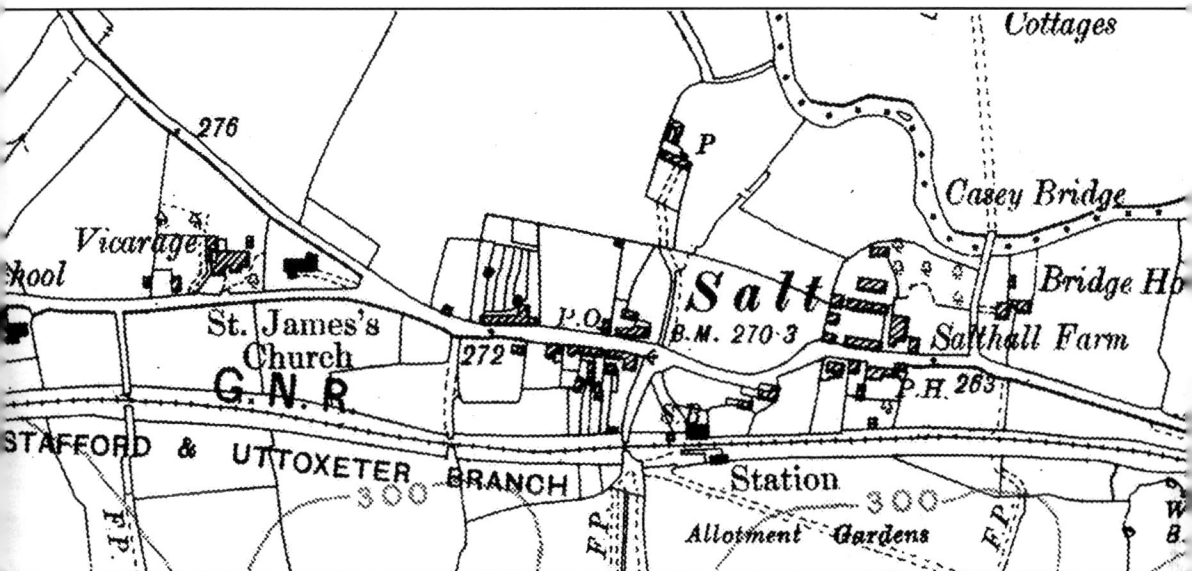

XXIX.   At 12ins to 1 mile is the 1938 edition and it shows no sidings. Some railway documents included the suffix '& SANDON' to reduce confusion with the nearby NSR station, which had the names in the reverse order.

90.   The only view we have seen is this glimpse from the SLS train in 1957. There had been no need for a signal box here. A salt works was to be found east of Stafford for many years, as well as those at the next station. (H.C.Casserley)

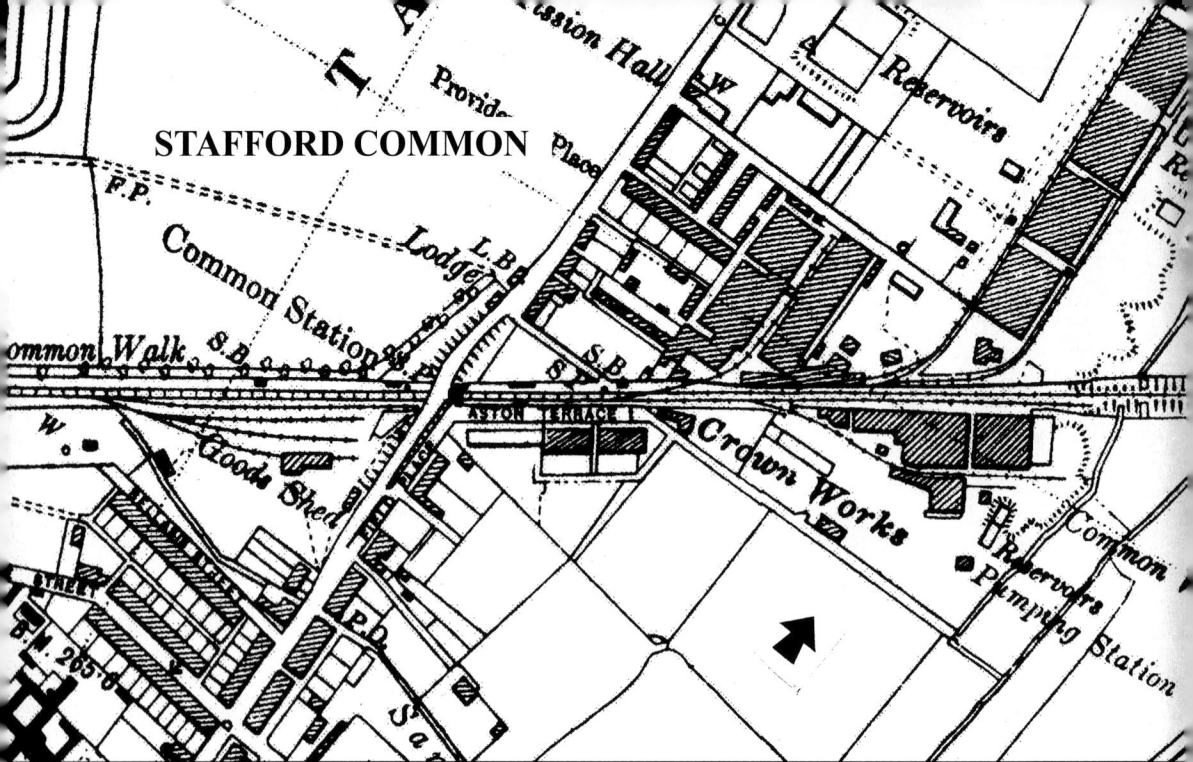

STAFFORD COMMON

XXX.    The 1938 survey is seen at 12ins to 1 mile. The station opened later than the others on the route, on 1st July 1874. It was west of the bridge until 1886, when the line was doubled from Stafford as far as here. The power station was built just beyond the right border.

91.    A 1952 view northeast from under the booking hall includes two works. Their owners were listed in 1938 as Manger's Salt Works Ltd and Stafford Salt & Alkali Co. Ltd. On the approach to Stafford were private sidings for Universal Grinding Wheel Ltd and Stafford Corporation's Gas Works. Its Electric Light Works had its own siding, nearby. (R.M.Casserley coll.)

92.   Also seen in the background of the previous picture is the 35-lever box, which became a ground frame in 1953. This and the next picture are from the SLS train, in 1957. Public goods traffic continued here until 5th August 1968. The yard had a 10-ton crane. (R.M.Casserley)

93.   We cross from single to double track on the same day and see the elevated booking office, which had not been used since the outbreak of war in 1939. Soon after, the RAF established sidings northeast of the station. They were in use until December 1952. The southern end of the route was used by the engineers during the electrification of the main line. (R.M.Casserley)

XXXI. Our route comes in at the top border of this 1921 survey at 6ins to 1 mile. Branching from it is the long siding to the gas works. South of the first junction is Castle Engine Works, birth place of the Bagnall locomotives.

STAFFORD

FOREGATE

STAFFORD ST

CASTLETOWN

ROWLEY PARK

Rowley Hall

Rowley Bank House

Trent Valley Junction

King Edward VI Grammar School

COUNTY MENTAL HOSPITAL

HIS MAJESTY'S PRISON

GENERAL INFIRMARY

Gas Works (Stafford Corporation)

Castle Engine Works

Station

Sorting Office

Green Bridge

Goods Sta.

Police Barracks

Friars' Cottage

CEMETERY

94. This postcard view is of platform 1, from which London trains departed. GNR trains for Uttoxeter used a bay platform at the far end of it. There were two through lines devoid of roofing. These structures date from 1861-62. (A.Dudman coll.)

95. Leaving to run via Salt and Uttoxeter to Derby Friarsgate in the mid-1920s is LNER class J3 0-6-0 no. 3177. Photos of regular trains on this route are rare. (A.Dudman coll.)

96.   Part of the massive locomotive depot is seen on 30th April 1933. The pitched roofing lasted until 1947 and the shed code became 5C for its final years, until closure in July 1965. No. 3379 was an ex-LNER class J3 0-6-0. (H.C.Casserley)

97.   Here is the front of the SLS train run on 23rd March 1957 and seen several times earlier. No. 41224 is a class 2MT 2-6-2T and is waiting at the former GNR bay platform, at the north end of the station. (A.Dudman coll.)

98. Newport Road bridge was a good place to view trains departing south. A rebuilt "Royal Scot" 4-6-0 class 7P waits to leave for Euston from platform 1 in 1958. On the left is the No.6 Box, plus the massive coaling tower, near the engine sheds. (E.Talbot/I.Pell coll.)

---

**For other views, see our** *Stafford to Wellington* **(pictures 1-15),** *Wolverhampton to Stafford* **(111-120),** *Stafford to Chester* **(1-18) and** *Rugby to Stafford* **(102-120) albums.**

---

99. Looking south from the next bridge on 2nd April 1960 we can enjoy Trent Valley Junction. The Rugby lines are on the left and those to Wolverhampton are on the right. Electric traction to Lichfield began on 22nd October 1963 and to Wolverhampton on 16th August 1965. Signalling of the area was taken over by Rugby Rail Operating Centre on 1st September 2015. (R.Shenton/I.Pell)

100. Electric operation from Crewe began on 7th January 1963. Here no. 86401 waits to leave for London in May 1987. It was unusual to be in Network South East colours on this route. It was the only one of its class to be so treated. (P.Jones)

101. It is May 1998 and we witness no. 37418 *East Lancashire Railway* about to depart with the 11.58 Birmingham New Street to Holyhead service. On the right is platform 7, which was dedicated to Royal Mail traffic. Nos 1, 6 and 7 had reversible running facilities. (P.Jones)

102. Seen on 21st February 2015 is a class 390 Pendolino unit, working the 10.47 Liverpool to Euston service. This was part of the first fleet to have tilting bodies. The station rebuilding took place in 1960-62. (P.Jones)

# 4. Cheadle Branch

XXXII.  Cheadle is top right on this 1947 map at 2ins to 1 mile. Tean had become a halt by then and is not shown, but the next map reveals its location. The disused tunnel is annotated and the original route is marked at each end of it. The terminus is near the right border and somewhat isolated from Cheadle. Close to most of the left border is the entire route of the 1893 Foxfield Railway. Although

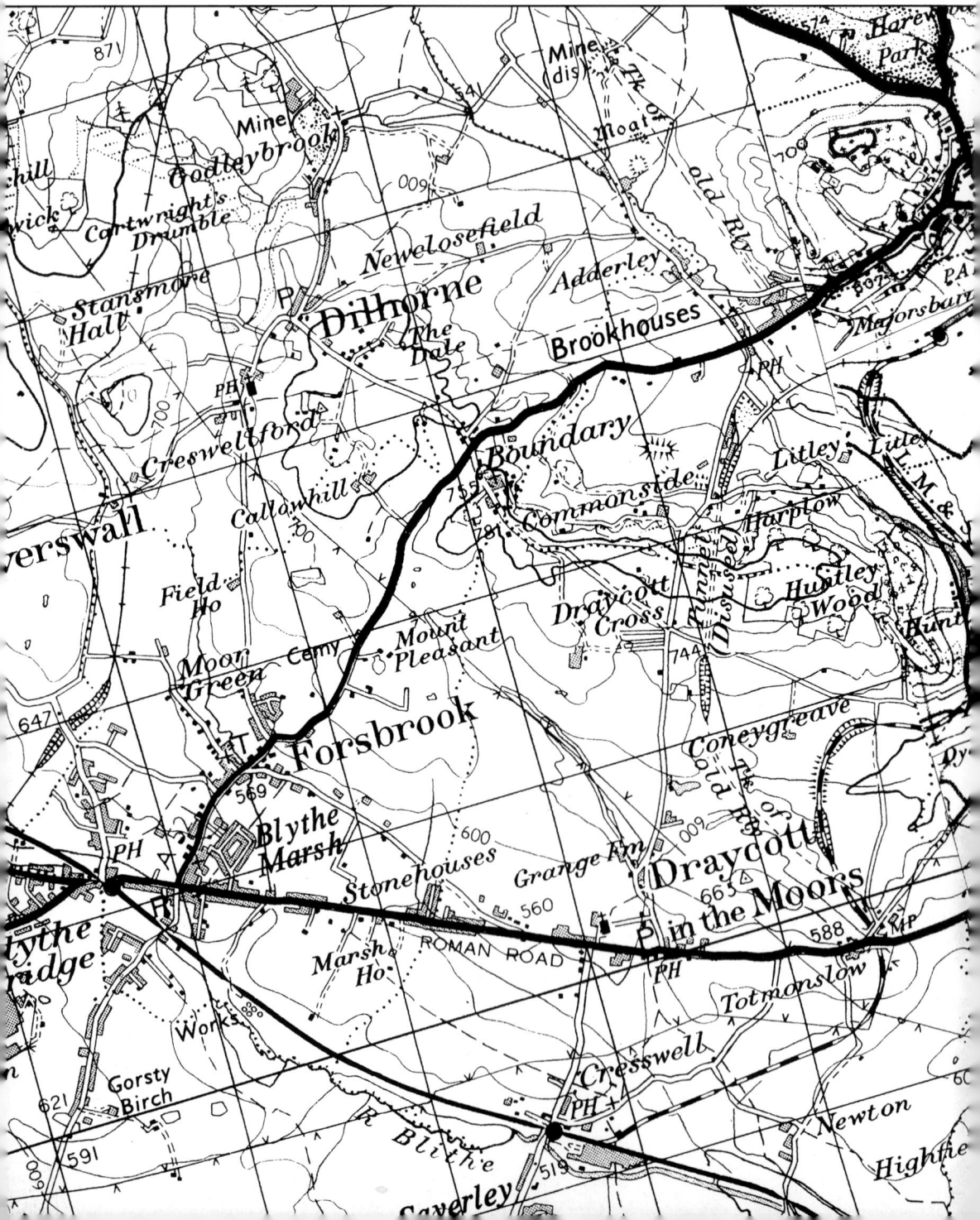

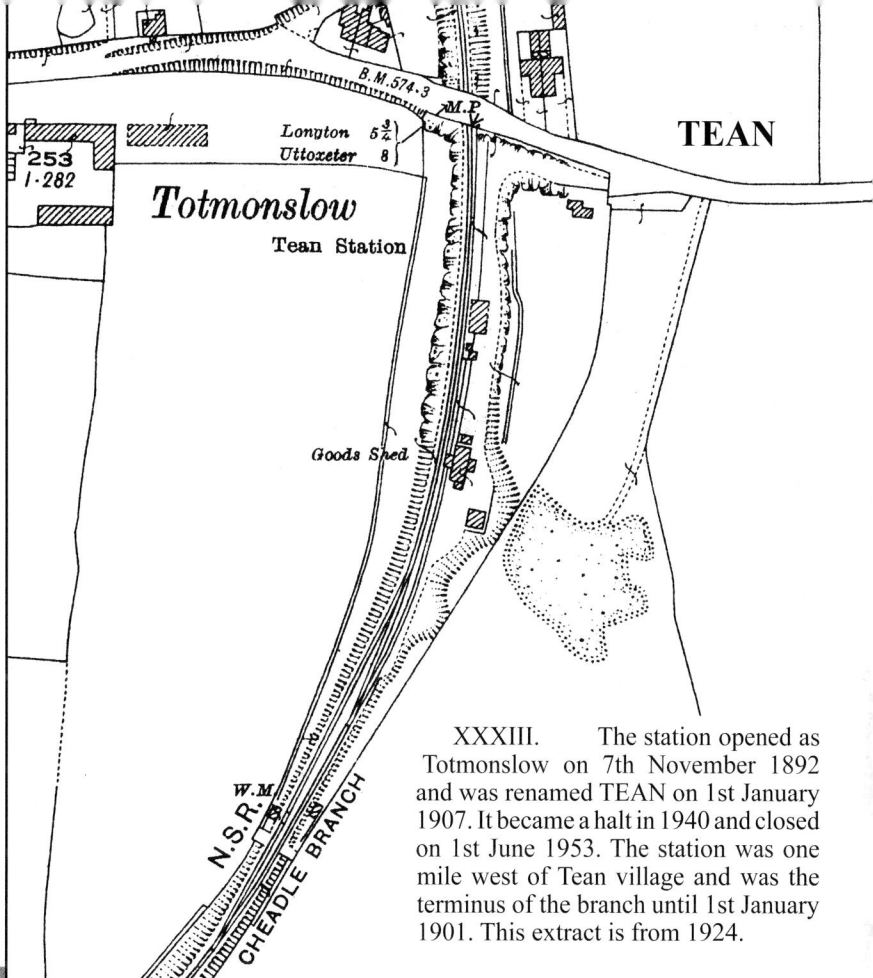

**TEAN**

B.M.574.3

M.P

Longton 5¼
Uttoxeter 8

253
1·282

*Totmonslow*

Tean Station

*Goods Shed*

W.M.

N.S.R.

CHEADLE BRANCH

seen to end close to Godleybrook, the pit was called Foxfield Colliery (closed 1965). The disused mine and track, top right, were associated with Parkhall Colliery (closed 1930). Just north of the tunnel is a connection to New Hadden Colliery (closed 1943). Cheadle Tunnel collapsed for 400ft of its length on 2nd November 1918, due to mine settlement below it. The new circuitous route is near the right border. Temporary supports were in place by 28th November of that year, but the fresh line was not opened until 26th November 1933. One bridge had collapsed during its construction and a weak embankment gave way.

XXXIII.    The station opened as Totmonslow on 7th November 1892 and was renamed TEAN on 1st January 1907. It became a halt in 1940 and closed on 1st June 1953. The station was one mile west of Tean village and was the terminus of the branch until 1st January 1901. This extract is from 1924.

103.    Red sandstone was widespread near the surface, with coal not far below. This southward view is from near the bridge carrying the A50 over the line. The NSR operated the trains from the outset, these running to and from Turntall, in most cases. (LOSA)

104. The village was noted for tape weaving from 1747. The large mill was eventually converted to flats. This northward record confirms that milk transport and chocolate vending took place here. This building was erected by the NSR, soon after it acquired the line in 1907. It came in flat-pack form from Keele Park, but the closets and urinals were not available until July 1909. (LOSA)

105. The disused platform is seen on 6th March 1958. The goods yard had also closed on 1st May 1953, but the goods shed is still evident. A good bus service was available on the main road. (H.F.Wheeller/R.S.Carpenter)

# CHEADLE

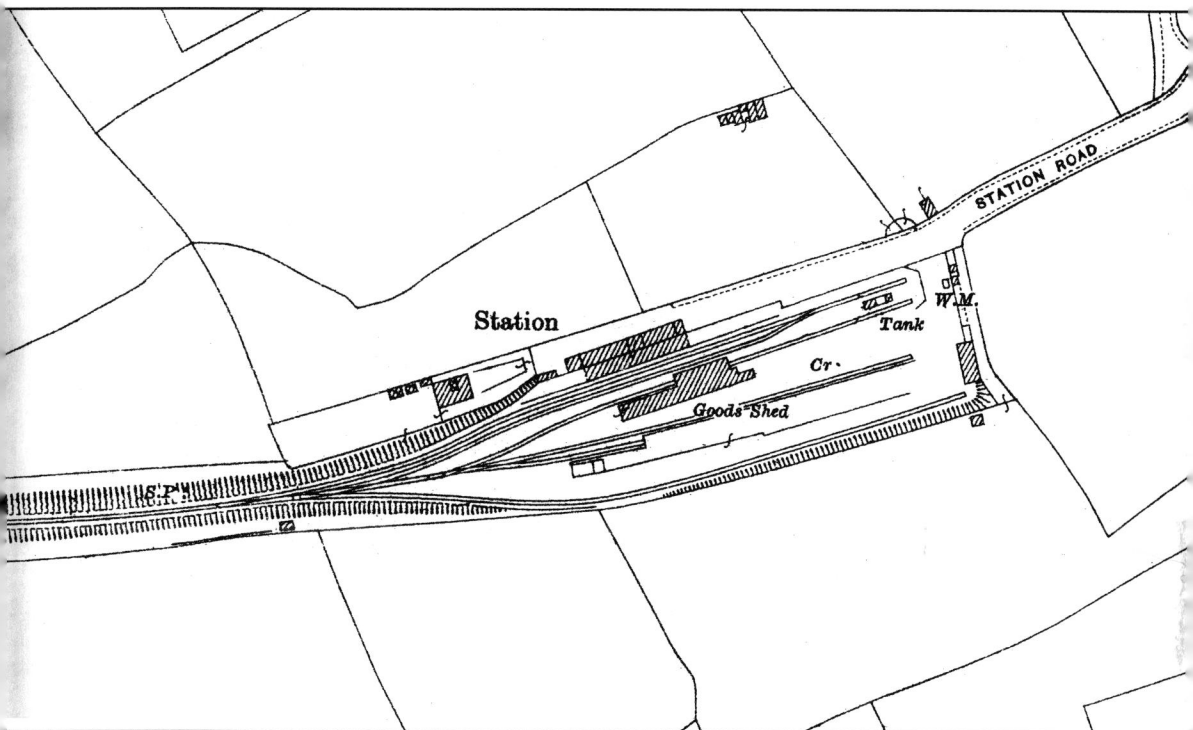

XXXIV.   The 1924 edition confirms the remoteness of this station from the town, which had 5186 residents in 1901 and 8010 in 1961.

106.   Standing at the first station is a four-wheeled NSR compartment coach being uncoupled from a Manning Wardle 0-6-0ST. This probably belonged to a contractor. (A.Dudman coll.)

107.    As at Tean, the first building was temporary and the one illustrated was completed by the NSR in 1910. Seen on 30th May 1935 is LMS class 3P 2-6-2T no. 76, a type introduced that year. They were reclassifield 3MT in 1948. (R.S.Carpenter coll.)

108.    The goods shed was also finished in 1910, but is seen better in the next views. Pictured on 22nd May 1948 is ex-LMS 2-6-4T no. 42585, which was based at Stoke Shed. It is working the 6.30pm to Cresswell. Some Wakes Week holiday trains terminated here in the 1950s. (W.A.Camwell/SLS)

109.    There was no signal box, the branch being worked on the "One engine in steam" system. This panorama was recorded on 6th March 1958. A new road-rail loading dock replaced use of the goods shed in the late 1960s. The yard had a 10-ton crane and was open to public traffic until 8th March 1978. The branch closed for mineral traffic on 10th March 1986. (H.F.Wheeller/R.S.Carpenter)

110.    The water tank is still present on 22nd October 1960, as a DMU waits to leave for Stoke-on-Trent at 1.35pm. Sand was the main traffic in the final years, around 1200 tons per day often leaving. It was loaded from lorries at a dock built on the site of the goods shed. The last passenger left on 17th June 1963. Part of the route was retained by the civil engineers until 1986. Apart from the house once used by the station master, all was cleared in 1994 to make way for a housing estate. (E.Wilmshurst)

# 5. Foxfield Railways

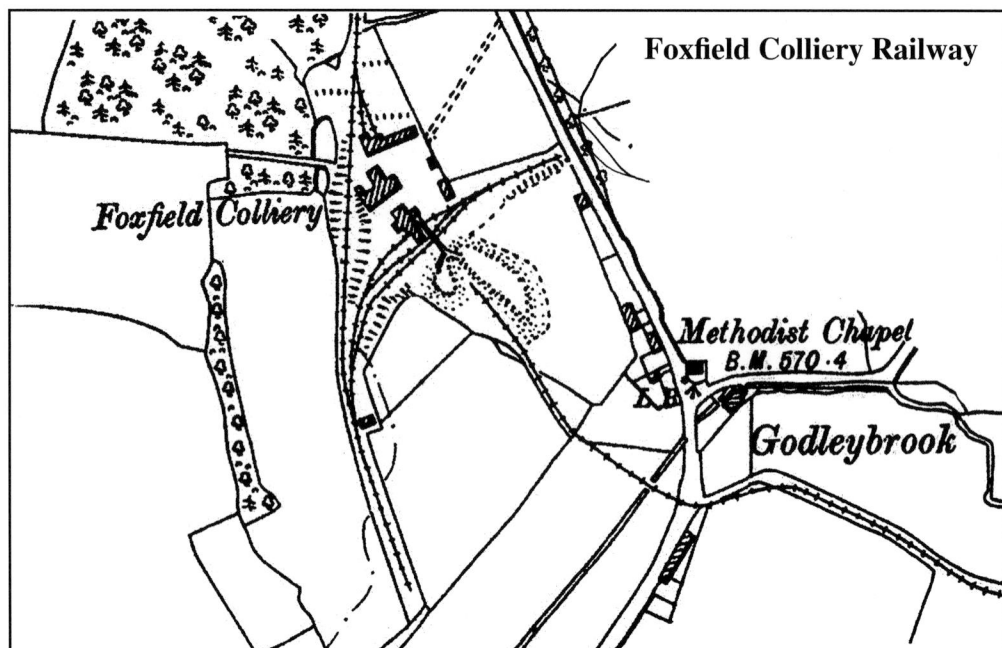

**Foxfield Colliery Railway**

XXXV.     The 1898 survey at 6ins to 1 mile can be located top left of map no. XXXII of 1947, which follows picture 102. The tramway on the right was already out of use. The route at the top continued on a semicircular alignment, to then run south to Blythe Bridge.

111. The first mine shaft was completed in September 1888, although coal had been dug near the surface for decades. The rail connection to Blythe Bridge station was brought into use in February 1893 and the first locomotive was this Hudswell Clarke 0-6-0ST *Foxfield*. It ran on its own until 1900. (V.J.Bradley/A.Neale)

112. By 1923, the output was over 50,000 tons per annum and in 1927 it was combined with Park Hall, but the latter closed in 1930. Foxfield's production ceased in August 1965 and much of the area was acquired by Tean Minerals for other products. Here is a train with wagons showing Park Hall & Foxfield, headed by *Excelsior* in the early 1930s. The 0-6-0ST was from Kerr Stuart in 1900 and retired in 1948. (A.Dudman coll.)

## Foxfield Light Railway

113.    Informal operation through rural conditions was necessary in the early years, as witnessed on 28th July 1974. The Caverswall Road station was built on a new extension. Bagnall 0-6-0ST no. 2193 *Topham* of 1922 will terminate close to the former exchange sidings. (T.Heavyside)

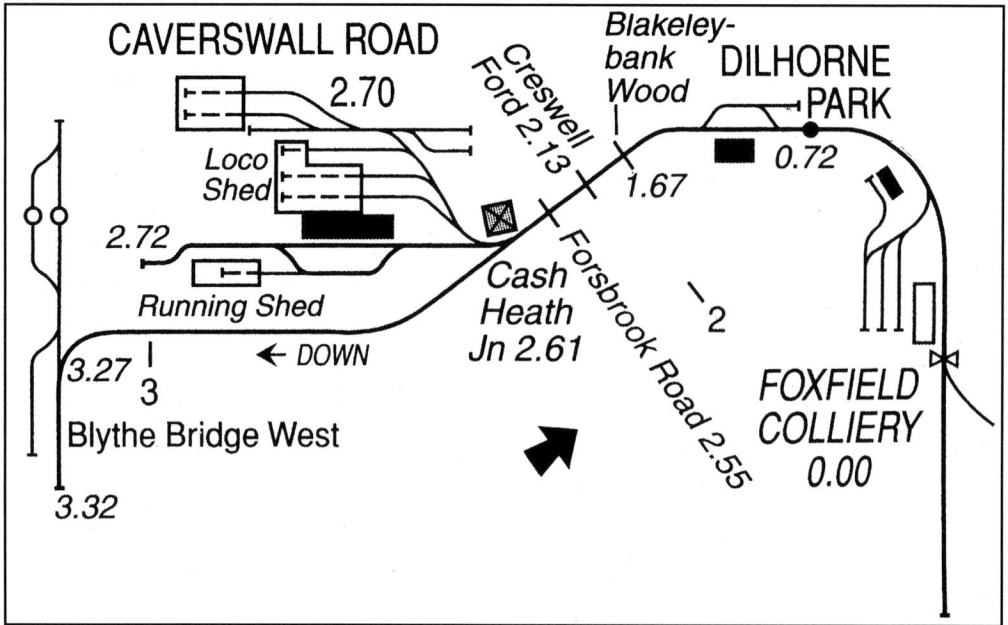

CAVERSWALL ROAD    2.70    Creswell Ford 2.13    Blakeley-bank Wood    DILHORNE PARK

Loco Shed    1.67    0.72

2.72

Running Shed    Cash Heath Jn 2.61    Forsbrook Road 2.55    2

3.27 / 3    ← DOWN

Blythe Bridge West    FOXFIELD COLLIERY    0.00

3.32

XXXVI. Tean Minerals did not require a railway and so a Society was formed and this is the track diagram by 2013. The mileage figures are from right to left. The main line connection was severed after closure. (©TRACKmaps)

114. Standing at the new terminus at Caverswall Road on 5th May 1986 is Hunslet "Austerity" no. 3839 of 1956. It will soon be uncoupled and go on to use the loop on the right. (T.Heavyside)

115.   A view from the other end of the platform reveals that the building is used to house locomotives. However, passengers are cared for at the far end. Ruston no. 408496 of 1957 is resting on 7th August 1988. (A.C.Hartless)

116.   An impressive display of industrial locomotives was on offer on 30th July 1995. Nearest are Peckett *No. 11*, built in 1911, and Barclay no. 2069 *Little Barford* of 1939. Both are 0-4-0STs. (T.Heavyside)

117. All aboard for Dilhorne Park on 7th August 1988. The fireman of "Austerity" 0-6-0ST *Wimblebury* collects the single line token to proceed along the line. The upper half of the signal box was originally at Hockley Crossing, Uttoxeter, and is now superimposed on a new build brick base. (A.C.Hartless)

**For details of train times contact Foxfield Railway on 01782 396210 or visit** *www.foxfieldrailway.co.uk.*

118. The line has a gradient of 1 in 51. It claims to be the steepest in Britain to haul passengers. Dilhorne Park is seen on 14th July 1974 as 0-4-0ST Bagnall no. 2623 *Hawarden* of 1940 waits in the siding. Arriving is Peckett 0-4-0ST, no. 933 *Henry Cort* of 1903. (T.Heavyside)

119.    We are at Dilhorne Park on 18th August 2007 and Ruston Hornsby 0-4-0DE no. 423657 of 1958 runs round the single coach of the 15.00 from Caverswall Road. (A.C.Hartless)

120.    This is the end of the line at Foxfield Colliery as it was on 28th July 1974, as Bagnall 0-6-0ST no. 2193 *Topham* of 1922 departs for Blythe Bridge sidings. We are near the colliery engine shed. On the left is Peckett 0-4-0ST no. 933 *Henry Cort* of 1903. (T.Heavyside)

MP **Middleton Press**

EVOLVING THE ULTIMATE RAIL ENCYCLOPEDIA

**Easebourne Midhurst GU29 9AZ. Tel:01730 813169**

www.middletonpress.co.uk email:info@middletonpress.co.uk

A-978 0 906520 B- 978 1 873793 C- 978 1 901706 D-978 1 904474 E - 978 1 906008 F - 978 1 908174

All titles listed below were in print at time of publication - please check current availability by looking at our website - *www.middletonpress.co.uk* or by requesting a Brochure which includes our *LATEST* RAILWAY TITLES also our TRAMWAY, TROLLEYBUS, MILITARY and COASTAL series

**A**

Abergavenny to Merthyr C 91 8
Abertillery & Ebbw Vale Lines D 84 5
Aberystwyth to Carmarthen E 90 1
Allhallows - Branch Line to A 62 8
Alton - Branch Lines to A 11 6
Andover to Southampton A 82 6
Ascot - Branch Lines around A 64 2
Ashburton - Branch Line to B 95 4
Ashford - Steam to Eurostar B 67 1
Ashford to Dover A 48 2
Austrian Narrow Gauge D 04 3
Avonmouth - BL around D 42 5
Aylesbury to Rugby D 91 3

**B**

Baker Street to Uxbridge D 90 6
Bala to Llandudno E 87 1
Banbury to Birmingham D 27 2
Banbury to Cheltenham E 63 5
Bangor to Holyhead F 01 7
Bangor to Portmadoc E 72 7
Barking to Southend C 80 2
Barmouth to Pwllheli E 53 6
Barry - Branch Lines around D 50 0
Bartlow - Branch Lines to F 27 7
Bath Green Park to Bristol C 36 9
Bath to Evercreech Junction A 60 4
Beamish 40 years on rails E94 9
Bedford to Wellingborough D 31 9
Berwick to Drem F 64 2
Berwick to St. Boswells F 75 8
B'ham to Tamworth & Nuneaton F 63 5
Birkenhead to West Kirby F 61 1
Birmingham to Wolverhampton E253
Bletchley to Cambridge D 94 4
Bletchley to Rugby E 07 9
Bodmin - Branch Lines around B 83 1
Boston to Lincoln F 80 2
Bournemouth to Evercreech Jn A 46 8
Bournemouth to Weymouth A 57 4
Bradshaw's History F18 5
Bradshaw's Rail Times 1850 F 13 0
Bradshaw's Rail Times 1895 F 11 6
Branch Lines series - see town names
Brecon to Neath D 43 2
Brecon to Newport D 16 6
Brecon to Newtown E 06 2
Brighton to Eastbourne A 16 1
Brighton to Worthing A 03 1
Bristol to Taunton D 03 6
Bromley South to Rochester B 23 7
Bromsgrove to Birmingham D 87 6
Bromsgrove to Gloucester D 73 9
Broxbourne to Cambridge F16 1
Brunel - A railtour D 74 6
Bude - Branch Line to B 29 9
Burnham to Evercreech Jn B 68 0

**C**

Cambridge to Ely D 55 5
Canterbury - BLs around B 58 9
Cardiff to Dowlais (Cae Harris) E 47 5
Cardiff to Pontypridd E 95 6
Cardiff to Swansea E 42 0
Carlisle to Hawick E 85 7
Carmarthen to Fishguard E 66 6
Caterham & Tattenham Corner B251
Central & Southern Spain NG E 91 8
Chard and Yeovil - BLs a C 30 7
Charing Cross to Dartford A 75 8
Charing Cross to Orpington A 96 3
Cheddar - Branch Line to B 90 9
Cheltenham to Andover C 43 7
Cheltenham to Redditch D 81 4
Chester to Birkenhead F 21 5
Chester to Manchester F 51 2
Chester to Rhyl E 93 2
Chester to Warrington F 40 6
Chichester to Portsmouth A 14 7
Clacton and Walton - BLs to F 04 8
Clapham Jn to Beckenham Jn B 36 7
Cleobury Mortimer - BLs a E 18 5
Clevedon & Portishead - BLs to D180
Consett to South Shields E 57 4
Cornwall Narrow Gauge D 56 2
Corris and Vale of Rheidol E 65 9
Craven Arms to Llandeilo E 35 2
Craven Arms to Wellington E 33 8
Crawley to Littlehampton A 34 5
Crewe to Manchester F 57 4
Cromer - Branch Lines around C 26 0
Croydon to East Grinstead B 48 0
Crystal Palace & Catford Loop B 87 1
Cyprus Narrow Gauge E 13 0

**D**

Darjeeling Revisited F 09 3
Darlington Leamside Newcastle E 28 4
Darlington to Newcastle D 98 2
Dartford to Sittingbourne B 34 3
Denbigh - Branch Lines around F 32 1
Derby to Stoke-on-Trent F 93 2
Derwent Valley - BL to the D 06 7
Devon Narrow Gauge E 09 3
Didcot to Banbury D 02 9
Didcot to Swindon C 84 0
Didcot to Winchester C 13 0
Dorset & Somerset NG D 76 0
Douglas - Laxey - Ramsey E 75 8
Douglas to Peel C 88 8
Douglas to Port Erin C 55 0
Douglas to Ramsey D 39 5
Dover to Ramsgate A 78 9
Dublin Northwards in 1950s E 31 4
Dunstable - Branch Lines to E 27 7

**E**

Ealing to Slough C 42 0
Eastbourne to Hastings A 27 7
East Cornwall Mineral Railways D 22 7
East Croydon to Three Bridges A 53 6
Eastern Spain Narrow Gauge E 56 7
East Grinstead - BLs to A 07 9
East Kent Light Railway A 61 1
East London - Branch Lines of C 44 4
East London Line B 80 0
East of Norwich - Branch Lines E 69 7
Effingham Junction - BLs a A 74 1
Ely to Norwich C 90 1
Enfield Town & Palace Gates D 32 6
Epsom to Horsham A 30 7
Eritrean Narrow Gauge E 38 3
Euston to Harrow & Wealdstone C 89 5
Exeter to Barnstaple B 15 2
Exeter to Newton Abbot C 49 9
Exeter to Tavistock B 69 5
Exmouth - Branch Lines to B 00 8

**F**

Fairford - Branch Line to A 52 9
Falmouth, Helston & St. Ives C 74 1
Fareham to Salisbury A 67 3
Faversham to Dover B 05 3
Felixstowe & Aldeburgh - BL to D 20 3
Fenchurch Street to Barking C 20 8
Festiniog - 50 yrs of enterprise C 83 3
Festiniog 1946-55 E 01 7
Festiniog in the Fifties B 68 8
Festiniog in the Sixties B 91 6
Ffestiniog in Colour 1955-82 F 25 3
Finsbury Park to Alexandra Pal C 02 8
French Metre Gauge Survivors F 88 8
Frome to Bristol B 77 0

**G**

Galashiels to Edinburgh F 52 9
Gloucester to Bristol D 35 7
Gloucester to Cardiff D 66 1
Gosport - Branch Lines around A 36 9
Greece Narrow Gauge D 72 2

**H**

Hampshire Narrow Gauge D 36 4
Harrow to Watford D 14 2
Harwich & Hadleigh - BLs to F 02 4
Harz Revisited F 62 8
Hastings to Ashford A 37 6
Hawick to Galashiels F 36 9
Hawkhurst - Branch Line to A 66 6
Hayling - Branch Line to A 12 3
Hay-on-Wye - BL around D 92 0
Haywards Heath to Seaford A 28 4
Hemel Hempstead - BLs to D 88 3
Henley, Windsor & Marlow - BLa C77 2
Hereford to Newport D 54 8
Hertford & Hatfield - BLs a E 58 1
Hertford Loop E 71 0
Hexham to Carlisle D 75 3
Hexham to Hawick F 08 6
Hitchin to Peterborough D 07 4
Holborn Viaduct to Lewisham A 81 9
Horsham - Branch Lines to A 02 4
Huntingdon - Branch Line to A 93 2

**I**

Ilford to Shenfield C 97 0
Ilfracombe - Branch Line to B 21 3
Industrial Rlys of the South East A 09 3
Ipswich to Diss F 81 9
Ipswich to Saxmundham C 41 3
Isle of Wight Lines - 50 yrs C 12 3
Italy Narrow Gauge F 17 8

**K**

Kent Narrow Gauge C 45 1
Kettering to Nottingham F 82-6
Kidderminster to Shrewsbury E 10 9
Kingsbridge - Branch Line to C 98 7
Kings Cross to Potters Bar E 62 8
King's Lynn to Hunstanton F 58 1
Kingston & Hounslow Loops A 83 3
Kingswear - Branch Line to C 17 8

**L**

Lambourn - Branch Line to C 70 3
Launceston & Princetown - BLs C 19 2
Leicester to Burton F 85 7
Lewisham to Dartford A 92 5
Lincoln to Cleethorpes F 56 7
Lines around Wimbledon B 75 6
Liverpool Street to Chingford D 01 2
Liverpool Street to Ilford C 34 5
Llandeilo to Swansea E 46 8
London Bridge to Addiscombe B 20 6
London Bridge to East Croydon A 58 1
Longmoor - Branch Lines to A 41 3
Looe - Branch Line to C 22 2
Loughborough to Nottingham F 68 0
Lowestoft - BLs around E 40 6
Ludlow to Hereford E 14 7
Lydney - Branch Lines around E 26 0
Lyme Regis - Branch Line to A 45 1
Lynton - Branch Line to B 04 6

**M**

Machynlleth to Barmouth E 54 3
Maesteg and Tondu Lines E 06 2
Majorca & Corsica Narrow Gauge F 41 3
March - Branch Lines around B 09 1
Market Drayton - BLs around F 67 3
Market Harborough to Newark F 86 4
Marylebone to Rickmansworth D 49 4
Melton Constable to Yarmouth Bch E031
Midhurst - Branch Lines of E 78 9
Midhurst - Branch Lines to F 00 0
Minehead - Branch Line to A 80 2
Mitcham Junction Lines B 01 5
Monmouth - Branch Lines to E 20 8
Monmouthshire Eastern Valleys D 71 5
Moretonhampstead - BL to C 27 7
Moreton-in-Marsh to Worcester D 26 5
Morpeth to Bellingham F 87 1
Mountain Ash to Neath D 80 7

**N**

Newark to Doncaster F 78 9
Newbury to Westbury C 66 6
Newcastle to Hexham D 69 2
Newport (IOW) - Branch Lines to A 26 0
Newquay - Branch Lines to C 71 0
Newton Abbot to Plymouth C 60 4
Newtown to Aberystwyth E 41 3
Northampton to Peterborough F 92 5
North East German NG D 44 9
Northern Alpine Narrow Gauge F 37 6
Northern France Narrow Gauge C 75 8
Northern Spain Narrow Gauge E 83 3
North London Line B 94 7
North of Birmingham F 55 0
North Woolwich - BLs around C 65 9
Nottingham to Boston F 70 3
Nottingham to Lincoln F 43 7

**O**

Ongar - Branch Line to E 05 5
Orpington to Tonbridge B 03 9
Oswestry - Branch Lines around E 60 4
Oswestry to Whitchurch E 81 9
Oxford to Bletchley D 57 9
Oxford to Moreton-in-Marsh D 15 9

**P**

Paddington to Ealing C 37 6
Paddington to Princes Risborough C819
Padstow - Branch Line to B 54 1
Pembroke and Cardigan - BLs to F 29 1
Peterborough to Kings Lynn E 32 1
Peterborough to Lincoln F 89 5
Peterborough to Newark F 72 7
Plymouth - BLs around B 98 5
Plymouth to St. Austell C 63 5
Pontypool to Mountain Ash D 65 4
Pontypridd to Merthyr F 14 7
Pontypridd to Port Talbot E 86 4
Porthmadog 1954-94 - BLa B 31 2
Portmadoc 1923-46 - BLa B 13 8
Portsmouth to Southampton A 31 4
Portugal Narrow Gauge E 67 3
Potters Bar to Cambridge D 70 8
Princes Risborough - BL to D 05 0
Princes Risborough to Banbury C 85 7

**R**

Railways to Victory C 16 1
Reading to Basingstoke B 27 5
Reading to Didcot C 79 6
Reading to Guildford A 47 5
Redhill to Ashford A 73 4
Return to Blaenau 1970-82 C 64 2
Rhyl to Bangor F 15 4
Rhymney & New Tredegar Lines E 48 2
Rickmansworth to Aylesbury D 61 6
Romania & Bulgaria NG E 23 9
Romneyrail C 32 1
Ross-on-Wye - BLs around E 30 7
Ruabon to Barmouth E 84 0
Rugby to Birmingham E 37 6
Rugby to Loughborough F 12 3
Rugby to Stafford F 07 9
Rugeley to Stoke-on-Trent F 90 1
Ryde to Ventnor A 19 2

**S**

Salisbury to Westbury B 39 8
Sardinia and Sicily Narrow Gauge F 50 5
Saxmundham to Yarmouth C 69 7
Saxony & Baltic Germany Revisited F 71 0
Saxony Narrow Gauge D 47 0
Seaton & Sidmouth - BLs to A 95 6
Selsey - Branch Line to A 04 8
Sheerness - Branch Line to B 16 2
Shenfield to Ipswich E 96 3
Shrewsbury - Branch Line to A 86 4
Shrewsbury to Chester E 70 3
Shrewsbury to Crewe F 48 2
Shrewsbury to Ludlow E 21 5
Shrewsbury to Newtown E 29 1
Sierra Leone Narrow Gauge D 28 9
Sirhowy Valley Line E 12 3
Sittingbourne to Ramsgate A 90 1
Skegness & Mablethorpe - BL to F 84 0
Slough to Newbury C 56 7
South African Two-foot gauge E 51 2
Southampton to Bournemouth A 42 0
Southend & Southminster BLs E 76 5
Southern Alpine Narrow Gauge F 22 2
Southern France Narrow Gauge C 47 5
South London Line B 46 6
South Lynn to Norwich City F 03 1
Southwold - Branch Line to A 15 4
Spalding - Branch Lines around E 52 9
Spalding to Grimsby F 65 9 6
Stafford to Chester F 34 5
Stafford to Wellington F 59 8
St Albans to Bedford D 08 1
St. Austell to Penzance C 67 3
St. Boswell to Berwick F 44 4
Steaming Through Isle of Wight A 56 7
Steaming Through West Hants A 69 7
Stourbridge to Wolverhampton E 16 1
St. Pancras to Barking D 68 5
St. Pancras to Folkestone E 88 8
St. Pancras to St. Albans C 78 9
Stratford to Cheshunt F 53 6
Stratford-u-Avon to Birmingham D777
Stratford-u-Avon to Cheltenham C253
Sudbury - Branch Lines to F 19 2
Surrey Narrow Gauge C 87 1
Sussex Narrow Gauge C 68 0
Swanage to 1999 - BL to A 33 8
Swanley to Ashford B 45 9
Swansea - Branch Lines around F 38 3
Swansea to Carmarthen E 59 8
Swindon to Bristol C 96 3
Swindon to Gloucester D 46 3
Swindon to Newport D 30 2
Swiss Narrow Gauge C 94 9

**T**

Talyllyn 60 E 98 7
Tamworth to Derby F 76 5
Taunton to Barnstaple B 60 2
Taunton to Exeter C 82 6
Taunton to Minehead F 39 0
Tavistock to Plymouth B 88 6
Tenterden - Branch Line to A 21 5
Three Bridges to Brighton A 35 2
Tilbury Loop C 86 4
Tiverton - BLs around C 62 8
Tivetshall to Beccles D 41 8
Tonbridge to Hastings A 44 4
Torrington - Branch Lines to B 37 4
Towcester - BLs around E 39 0
Tunbridge Wells BLs A 32 1

**U**

Upwell - Branch Line to B 64 0

**V**

Victoria to Bromley South A 98 7
Victoria to East Croydon A 40 6
Vivarais Revisited E 08 6

**W**

Walsall Routes F 45 1
Wantage - Branch Line to D 25 8
Wareham to Swanage 50 yrs D098
Waterloo to Windsor A 54 3
Waterloo to Woking A 38 3
Watford to Leighton Buzzard D 45 6
Wellingborough to Leicester F 73 4
Welshpool to Llanfair E 49 9
Wenford Bridge to Fowey C 09 3
Westbury to Bath B 55 8
Westbury to Taunton C 76 5
West Cornwall Mineral Rlys D 48 7
West Croydon to Epsom B 08 4
West German Narrow Gauge D 93 7
West London - BLs of C 50 5
West London Line B 84 8
West Wiltshire - BLs of D 12 8
Weymouth - BLs A 65 9
Willesden Jn to Richmond B 71 8
Wimbledon to Beckenham C 58 1
Wimbledon to Epsom B 62 6
Wimborne - BLs around A 97 0
Wisbech - BLs around C 01 7
Witham & Kelvedon - BLs a E 82 6
Woking to Alton A 59 8
Woking to Portsmouth A 25 3
Woking to Southampton A 55 0
Wolverhampton to Shrewsbury E444
Wolverhampton to Stafford F 79 6
Worcester to Birmingham D 97 5
Worcester to Hereford D 38 8
Worthing to Chichester A 06 2
Wrexham to New Brighton F 47 5
Wroxham - BLs around F 31 4

**Y**

Yeovil - 50 yrs change C 38 3
Yeovil to Dorchester A 76 5
Yeovil to Exeter A 91 8
York to Scarborough F 23 9